Praise for *A Place f*

Finally. I've been waiting for a book about wh[...] in Christ that adeptly works through the pertinent texts with sound scholarship, simplicity, a lack of agenda, and a love for the gospel, and finally, here it is. Not only do I love how Kendra adeptly explains and applies the Scriptures, I love the vision she presents for what it looks like for men and women to live out all that it means to be an integral part of His kingdom work in the world.

NANCY GUTHRIE, author and Bible teacher

This is the book I have been waiting for—for myself, for my daughters, for my friends. Reading it was like sitting down with a wise sister in the faith and diving deeply into what the Bible says about us as women. It turns out, contrary to many narratives in our world (and sometimes in the church), women are created with dignity, value, and essential purposes in the spheres where God has placed us. There is a place for you—a necessary role for every one of us—in our homes, in our churches, in our culture. Kendra Dahl writes with clarity, conviction, and compassion and I genuinely want every woman and teen girl I know to read this book.

JEN OSHMAN, author, speaker, women's ministry leader

Kendra has written a deeply thoughtful and gospel-rich book that invites women to engage Scripture with both conviction and courage. With clarity, warmth, and theological depth, *A Place for You* shows how God's grace speaks directly into the questions many women carry about value, vocation, and belonging in the church. This is a wise and faithful resource for women seeking to live before God with integrity—and for pastors who want to care well for the women in their congregations.

JUSTIN S. HOLCOMB, bishop, author, and seminary professor

Womanhood is frequently defined by culture, experience, or tradition, but Kendra challenges the reader to define it biblically. Her warm and honest style set a gracious tone to wrestle through rich passages on womanhood that have often been maligned or misapplied. *A Place for You* is a gift to the church.

> **KAREN HODGE**, Coordinator of Women's Ministries for the Presbyterian Church in America (PCA) and the author of *Transformed: Lifetaker to Life-giver* and *Life-giving Leadership*

Few issues in contemporary Christianity are as controversial and emotionally charged as those concerning the personal significance, role, and "place" of women, the daughters of the King. In *A Place for You*, Kendra Dahl has given God's family (Jesus' sisters *and* brothers) a "reframing" of the conversation that flows from reverence for and careful interpretation of God's Word; is discerningly conversant with cultural pressures; celebrates God's grace in Christ; and brims with transparency, realism, humor, and wisdom—all drawn from the joys and struggles of everyday life in home and church. You will come away from this book thinking, *Kendra is a sister who understands, whom I can trust, who loves Jesus, and who has helped me discover the "place" He has given me, where I can flourish for His glory*. You will be right.

> **DENNIS E. JOHNSON**, Professor Emeritus of Practical Theology, Westminster Seminary California; Assistant Pastor, Westminster Presbyterian Church, Dayton, TN

This book reflects the wisdom and insight I've seen firsthand from Kendra. I'm praying it will help more women find their place, and their voice, for the sake of flourishing, faithful churches.

> **COLLIN HANSEN**, vice president of content and editor in chief of The Gospel Coalition; host of the *Gospelbound* podcast

It's not just Adam, but the male-female relationship that is nuclear to human identity in Genesis 2–3. Kendra Dahl explores the deep structures of this biblical worldview in ways that challenge as well as support classic exegesis. This is precisely the kind of work that we need today for a richer and more biblical understanding of "womanhood."

> **MICHAEL HORTON**, J. Gresham Machen Professor of Theology, Westminster Seminary California

With a combination of careful biblical interpretation and insight from the reservoirs of experience, Kendra Dahl offers a compelling vision for God's plan and purpose for women. Anyone who doubts that traditional Christianity can and should honor women's vocations to serve Christ and His church will find this work consistently refreshing. Although Dahl addresses a female audience specifically, this book is filled with a Christian wisdom that is edifying for the rest of us as well.

DAVID VANDRUNEN, Robert B. Strimple Professor of Systematic Theology and Christian Ethics, Westminster Seminary California

The competing demands of cultural pressure, personal ambition, and biblical expectation can leave many Christian women confused about their purpose in the world. In this book, Kendra Dahl addresses all three with compassionate clarity, providing us with a rich biblical theology not only of womanhood, but of Christian identity and community. I would be pleased if every woman in my congregation read this fine contribution to an important discussion.

JONATHAN LANDRY CRUSE, husband, father, pastor, author

Thoroughly biblical, refreshingly reasonable, and deeply encouraging. I finished this book feeling so grateful for where God has placed me.

GLENNA MARSHALL, author of *Everyday Faithfulness*, *Memorizing Scripture*, and *Known and Loved*

Read this book and share it! While Kendra Dahl's *A Place for You* may focus on women, it will benefit anyone who wants to know the whole body of Christ better. It is a great combination of solid biblical teaching and godly wisdom delivered with wit and humor (and even tears). During her time at seminary, I had the pleasure of getting to know Kendra and her passion for the care and role of women in the church. There are students who are not only a joy to have in the classroom but also help you grow in your own understanding. Kendra is one of them. This book is the culmination of years of study and reflection and worthy of your time. Kendra is not afraid to raise difficult questions, and even if you do not agree with everything, the serious engagement will deepen your own understanding.

JOSHUA J. VAN EE, Associate Professor of Hebrew and Old Testament, Westminster Seminary California

Given the cultural landscape where words like complementarianism and egalitarianism are used to sort Christians into warring tribes, Kendra Dahl has written a warm, winsome, and theologically astute book on women's worth and roles. Always placing Christ and His kingdom at the center, Dahl reminds women that they have a valued place in the household of God. In doing so, Dahl reminds us that the bigger story— the redemptive arc of Christ's life, death, resurrection, and ascension— is our defining story. Several parts made me teary as I was reminded about the goodness of God for women. This will be a book I share with my congregation and my daughter.

ASHLEY HALES, Editorial Director for Print at *Christianity Today*; coauthor of *A Fruitful Life* (a Bible study on the Sermon on the Mount), *A Spacious Life*, and *Finding Holy in the Suburbs*

A Place for You weaves together biblical and covenant theology with great writing. Kendra has a heart to serve the church, and I was blessed to labor alongside her during the time she served as our church's Women's Ministry Coordinator. She's written something that thoughtfully engages with the text of Scripture while asking relevant questions pertaining to the image of God, gender, callings, and church ministry. Kendra's gracious and doctrinally sound approach is needed at a time when conversations about women's roles can generate more heat than light, or be avoided altogether.

ADRIEL SANCHEZ, pastor, North Park Presbyterian Church

A PLACE FOR YOU

REFRAMING
*Christian
Womanhood*

KENDRA DAHL

Moody Publishers
CHICAGO

Copyright © 2025 by
KENDRA DAHL

All rights reserved. No part of this book may be reproduced in any form without permission in writing from the publisher, except in the case of brief quotations embodied in critical articles or reviews.

Scripture quotations are from the ESV® Bible (The Holy Bible, English Standard Version®), © 2001 by Crossway, a publishing ministry of Good News Publishers. Used by permission. All rights reserved. The ESV text may not be quoted in any publication made available to the public by a Creative Commons license. The ESV may not be translated in whole or in part into any other language.
Portions of the anecdotes on pages 146–147 and 150 have appeared at kendradahl.com.

All emphasis in Scripture has been added.

Edited by Pamela Joy Pugh
Cover and Interior Design: Koko Toyama

Library of Congress Cataloging-in-Publication Data

Names: Dahl, Kendra author
Title: A place for you : notes on a woman›s dignity, courage, and belonging
/ Kendra Dahl.
Description: Chicago, IL : Moody Publishers, [2025] | Includes
bibliographical references. | Summary: «We have human longings-to be
valued and understood, and to contribute in meaningful ways. This book
showcases God›s noble design, gives voice to women›s desires, and
encourages us to hold fast to truth. Dahl invites women to embrace their
dignity and delight that God made them female»-- Provided by publisher.
Identifiers: LCCN 2025012105 (print) | LCCN 2025012106 (ebook) | ISBN
9780802441157 paperback | ISBN 9780802469915 ebook
Subjects: LCSH: Christian women--Religious life | Dignity--Religious
aspects--Christianity | Courage--Religious aspects--Christianity |
BISAC: RELIGION / Christian Living / Women›s Interests | RELIGION /
Christian Living / Personal Growth
Classification: LCC BV4527 .D2433 2025 (print) | LCC BV4527 (ebook) | DDC
248.8/43--dc23/eng/20250605
LC record available at https://lccn.loc.gov/2025012105
LC ebook record available at https://lccn.loc.gov/2025012106

Originally delivered by fleets of horse-drawn wagons, the affordable paperbacks from D. L. Moody's publishing house resourced the church and served everyday people. Now, after more than 125 years of publishing and ministry, Moody Publishers' mission remains the same—even if our delivery systems have changed a bit. For more information on other books (and resources) created from a biblical perspective, go to www.moodypublishers.com or write to:

Moody Publishers
820 N. LaSalle Boulevard
Chicago, IL 60610

1 3 5 7 9 10 8 6 4 2

Printed in the United States of America

For my daughters.
May you know your God,
your own minds,
and that there's a place in the church for you.

Contents

Part 1: Conviction

Chapter 1: Beckoned | On Knowing Your God and
Your Own Mind   13

Chapter 2: Wanted | On Recognizing Your Value   25

Chapter 3: Storied | On Being Defined by Mercy   49

Chapter 4: Commissioned | On Doing Work That Matters 71

Part 2: Courage

Chapter 5: Vulnerable | On Being the Weaker Vessel   99

Chapter 6: Quiet | On Finding Your Voice   119

Chapter 7: Limited | On the Dignity of Being Human
(and the Joy of Forming a Village)   139

Chapter 8: Secondary | On Having a Place   163

Closing Thoughts | A Letter for My Daughters   189

Acknowledgments   197

Notes   201

PART I
Conviction

1

Beckoned

ON KNOWING YOUR GOD AND YOUR OWN MIND

"One thing is necessary. Mary has chosen the good portion, which will not be taken away from her."

JESUS, LUKE 10:42

On the eve of my seminary graduation, I stood before my professors, classmates, friends, and family and gave a speech reflecting on my time as a student. At a loss for how to sum up the joy and agony of those nearly four years of graduate school, I settled on a poem I wrote about what it was like to walk through those years as a woman. I called it "Your Mom Went to Seminary."

I started crafting the poem during one of my first classes, summer Greek, an intensive course that inaugurates most students' seminary training. It's six grueling weeks of Greek paradigms, daily quizzes, and anxious prayers the professor won't call on you for the next exercise. Class meets for the first couple of hours in the morning, takes a break, and then resumes in the afternoon. The pace is swift, the memorization unrelenting.

When my husband, Jordan, took summer Greek a year prior, I distracted myself with our three children (then four, five, and nine) in our new California home. We did zoo trips and beach days, ate cereal for dinner, and did our back-to-school shopping while Jordan stayed at the library until it closed and returned when it opened, doing his best to juggle class and work.

Your Mom Went to Seminary

The next summer it was my turn. Fortunately, we were entering the "arrival" stage of family life, where everyone could feed themselves breakfast, and all we had to do was yell, "Get ready to go!" and somehow, we managed to leave the house with everyone having shoes on. On top of that, it was summer vacation and Jordan worked from home. He could loosely supervise (as in, make sure the house didn't burn down) while our kids benefited from the group parenting that was seminary housing.

Nonetheless, my transition to student status was challenging. Despite Jordan's help and encouragement and the support we received from the village surrounding us, I never felt okay about spending my days at the library as my classmates did. Recalling our summertime adventures the year prior, my kids had expectations. So I crammed for quizzes at the crack of dawn, did as many Greek exercises as I could in my break between classes, and then raced home so we could get to the beach.

I WAS WORKING OUT THE REALITY OF BEING A CHRISTIAN WOMAN, SIFTING THROUGH TENSIONS THAT HAD BEEN DEVELOPING FOR SEVERAL YEARS.

Meanwhile, my classmates lamented their lack of time to properly study and prepare for class. I felt a bit bewildered as I pondered my own juggling act.

This is where the poem started. "Your Mom Went to Seminary" began as a list of ways my seminary experience differed from my peers. If I'm honest, it was rooted in resentment as I compared myself to my classmates, knowing that many were single and others had the support of wives who kept everything afloat while they gave all their time to studying.

But over time, I realized this list I had been documenting was about more than wanting my professors and peers to acknowledge my challenge of going to graduate school as a wife and mom of three children. It was me working out the reality of being a Christian woman, sifting through tensions that had been developing ever since I came to faith eight years earlier.

Though I Was Blind, Now I See

I entered the church as a single mom with a buried abortion story and a lot of questions. My childhood faith had floundered in college, and by the time I graduated, I was angry at God and done with His people. So when I stumbled back into a worship service a few years later, my two-year-old in tow, I expected to hate what I found there. Instead, I heard the gospel proclaimed in its simplicity and glory. It was like I'd never heard it before. I had "exchanged the truth about God for a lie," I realized (Rom. 1:25). But I also understood for the first time that there was nothing I could do to make up for the sins of my past, nor was there any need—Jesus paid the penalty for my sins in full (Col. 2:14), setting me free from any and all condemnation (Rom. 8:1) and granting me His record of perfect righteousness (2 Cor. 5:21).

NEW WOMAN, NEW EYES, NEW LEARNING

Maybe it goes without saying, but I never tire of telling this story: I was a new woman! I had so much to learn, but I felt like the blind man after he received sight: "One thing I do know, that though I was blind, now I see" (John 9:25). After years of trying to hold myself up, determined to protect myself and my daughter Hadley from the ways the Bible had been used to shame and stifle me, I found refuge in its pages. There, I beheld a wise and merciful God who orchestrated all of human history to accomplish salvation in His Son. I experienced His grace in tangible ways as Hadley and I were welcomed like family into a community of believers.

I was eager—but cautious. As I looked at the Bible with new eyes, I saw God's intense love and grace rather than disappointment and condemnation. It made me wonder what other ways I'd missed seeing God, settling instead for man's poor interpretation. I felt like I'd been lied to all my years in the church. Because of those feelings, I met every new claim about God or what the Bible said with some suspicion, requiring proof from my new Christ-centered understanding of the Scriptures. I noticed my questions—directed to women who stepped in to mentor me— were often passed along to more knowledgeable men. But I didn't want to lean on anyone else's Bible understanding. I wanted to forge my own. And I couldn't learn fast enough. I read and listened to everything I could get my hands on.

Along with learning, I jumped into the life of the church but found myself struggling to understand my value and contribution. My pastors meant well, but they believed focusing their efforts on discipling men and raising them up as leaders would necessarily result in care for the women. I felt silenced and unsure of my place, and I could see other women experiencing similar confusion. But our pastors taught the Scriptures and spoke of a beautiful complementarity between the sexes that stirred longing in my heart. I wanted to be protected, cared for, and cherished.

And, as the truth of the gospel transformed my heart, I also wanted to be prepared to do and be whatever He called me to. I needed to know what it meant to be a Christian, yes, but I was also deeply concerned about what it meant to be a Christian woman.

DISCERNING GODLY WOMANHOOD

In those first months of my discipleship, I found and learned from voices who confidently defined biblical womanhood in vocational terms. The godly woman embraces her high and holy calling as wife and mother, these writers taught me. They convinced me that embracing my God-given role was an act of defiance against a feminist culture seeking to rob me of my true femininity, and I strove to live up to this ideal. It was a bit of a challenge since, as a single mother, I had only half of the equation (and had gone about it in the wrong order). But after meeting and marrying my husband, I settled into my new role as a homemaker and went about having more babies.

OUR PASTOR SAT BEFORE THE CONGREGATION AND APOLOGIZED FOR THE WAYS HE HAD FAILED TO CARE FOR WOMEN AND VALUE THEIR GIFTS.

We didn't thrive. My babies were sweet and my husband is amazing. But I was depressed and a little bored, trying to be someone I wasn't. As Jordan and I began to revisit our early convictions about men's and women's roles, we lamented together the ways we had unnecessarily boxed each other in, creating rules where God gives freedom. We found new voices from people who shared our theological convictions, still esteeming womanhood but also creating space for a diversity of experiences and expressions. I was inspired by thoughtful women who loved God and the Scriptures and sought to serve His church faithfully.

So we started pressing in, asking our elders more questions and challenging the narratives and practices surrounding men and women. Eventually, our pastor sat before the congregation and apologized for the ways he had failed to care for women and value their gifts. He invited me to come alongside him to help create spaces for women to be heard, discipled, and serve our congregation.

Though my views had changed in some ways, my study of the Scriptures still persuaded me toward a version of what has been labeled "complementarianism," the belief that men and women are created by God with equal dignity and value, that God has called married men to lead their households, and that He has reserved the role of pastor/elder in the church for qualified men.

But those convictions didn't preclude me from believing God has a place for women like me—women who want to love Him with our minds as well as our hearts, who have a vision for meaningful vocations both inside and outside our homes, who want to serve the church in meaningful ways. And so, this mom went to seminary.

Rattled Identity

Seminary exposed something I hadn't wanted to admit: Before pursuing graduate school, I felt secure and validated in my role as a stay-at-home wife and mom. Despite my shifting convictions toward a more spacious expression of womanhood, the part-time job I worked serving the church only occupied the nooks and crannies of my time. I wrote in the morning hours and hosted Bible studies in my home during naptime. I leaned occasionally on babysitters but did my best to keep my ambitions from robbing my family of anything.

But when I started seminary, my identity was rattled. It was normal for seminary wives to audit an evening class or two, often with a nursing baby in arms. But to take the bold step of becoming a full-fledged student alongside my husband—to miss my kids' field trips and band concerts and feed my family another round of In-N-Out, all while betraying the fact that my ambitions stretched outside of our home—*that* was venturing onto shaky ground. I fielded questions from classmates about why I needed the education. "Do you hope to be a pastor?" some would ask, their misgivings obvious. (The answer is no.) My baggage from my early years in the church resurfaced as I tried to discern truth from error about biblical womanhood, the role of men and women in the church, and my calling as a woman.

MAKING IT PRACTICAL

I did more reading, but mostly I came up short. I struggled to find people who held to complementarian convictions alongside a practical vision for men and women partnering together in ministry. Conversations around these topics were vitriolic and racked with suspicion, quick to throw out the accusation of "feminist" or "liberal."

Though I was confident my education was valuable, I struggled to justify it to myself and others. Instead, I tried to make it work without costing my family too much, all the while feeling plagued with guilt over my many failures as a wife and mom. Meanwhile, my poem, "Your Mom Went to Seminary," continued to develop in my heart, evolving into a letter of apology. While we ate our takeout in the car with Greek songs playing in the background, I silently pleaded with my children not to hold this season against me. I desperately wanted them to understand.

But something remarkable happened during those years of seminary. Jordan finally confronted my guilt, refuting my assumptions that he resented my ambition. "Your education is just as important as mine," he would say as he offered to do the drive-thru run. We began to learn what partnership in marriage could look like, taking turns and propping each other up.

My professors respected me, welcoming my voice and painting a picture of the myriad ways women contribute to the church. My classmates and I sat around the fire debating the role of women and, over time, these became sharpening conversations for all of us—future pastors thinking deeply about how they could better care for women and leverage their gifts for the good of the church.

I began to dig into the passages of Scripture most often flung around during these debates, and what I found there was a renewed conviction regarding differentiated gender roles in the church, seeing behind them a God who is purposeful and wise and who created both men and women for His glory and each other's good.

As I worked through all these things, I started to see in my children glimpses of who God is shaping them to be. And suddenly it struck me: All this work God was doing in my heart—to soften the rough edges, to strengthen my faith, and to give me confidence in my calling as a woman in the church—wasn't robbing my children, it was *for* my children. Especially for my daughters. I want to raise them to know and experience what their dad and I have come to believe with our whole hearts: The church has a place for women who know their God and who know their own minds.

So, as I concluded my time as a student, I climbed the stairs to the podium and leaned into the microphone, looking my children in the eyes as I said, "Your mom went to seminary. And she's not sorry."

My Fear

The summer after graduation, a friend came to visit, and we spent many hours catching up late into the night. She was weary, facing a crisis of faith, and poised to leave the church altogether. She could no longer accept the God she'd been trained to believe in. She couldn't continue in a community that didn't value her voice. She was tired of feeling bound and silenced, and those who beckoned her to freedom became louder and more compelling.

I understood. I'd experienced those things too. But I was afraid the liberation she was being sold wouldn't actually set her free. I wasn't necessarily afraid she might change her views on women in the church; we can disagree there while still sharing orthodox faith. But the treatment she'd received as a woman in the church had caused her to doubt God's goodness. I was afraid she was in danger of missing the beauty, kindness, and mercy of God and His purposes for His people.

I WONDERED, HOW MANY WOMEN HAVE LOST SIGHT OF THEIR VALUE?

Our conversations that week left me wondering about how many women sit in the pew, weary like her. How many have believed the lie that they are a means to an end, only valuable as someone's wife or mother? How many have tried to offer their perspective or gifts only to feel stupid or silenced? How many have felt like an afterthought, something nonessential in God's economy? I wondered how many women have left their faith over these things. How many have mistaken the sin and failures of people for God's carelessness?

We live in a world that claims to value women while peddling false promises of freedom that hinder our flourishing. At some point, every woman will likely feel her vulnerability threatened or exploited. We'll feel the weight of trying to do it all and the guilt of falling short. We will feel like too much and not enough, lamenting the liability of our womanhood.

Some of us will belong to churches that preach the equal dignity of women but have no vision for their unique value and essential contribution. We will feel like second-class citizens, wrestling with where we belong.[1] We will grow weary of the scandals, injustice, and abuse.

We will long for a reckoning.

But we'll also be so tired.

As I left my friend that day, I wept for her. But I also wept for my daughters. And for myself—for all of us who are trying to be or raise faithful women in this fraught time and place. And then, since I was done writing that poem, I decided to write this book.

To Know Your God and Your Own Mind

I love to recall those early days of ministry in the church God used to draw me to Himself. As the new women's discipleship director, the first event I planned was a theology workshop. A hundred women showed up. Maybe that doesn't feel like a lot to you, but to me, it was momentous. As I partnered with my pastor and a team of godly women, our church culture began to shift toward one that celebrated women's necessary contributions and perspectives. We invited women to love God with their minds as well as their hearts, and they showed up hungry. It was remarkable to behold.

But as I watched those hundred women flood through the doors, I panicked. I had prepared to teach them about the freedom I'd experienced as I laid down the heavy burdens of trying to achieve some standard of womanhood beyond what Scripture prescribes. I was eager to proclaim the truth of the gospel, to invite women to live with me in light of Christ's work on our behalf. But suddenly, I felt inadequate for the task.

I withdrew, texting my husband: "I just want to hide in the bathroom."

His response? "Coram Deo."

Coram Deo means "before God's face." R. C. Sproul writes, "To live *coram Deo* is to live one's entire life in the presence of God, under the authority of God, to the glory of God."[2]

This is what it means to live as women of conviction.

And it's also become our family definition of courage.

I have two goals for this book: I want to help you form conviction, and I want to instill courage. I want you to know your God, and I want you to know your own mind.

CORAM DEO

We live in an age where conflicting narratives clamor for our allegiance. And if we're going to stand firm on God's truth, we have to know what it is. We need to know our God. We need to know His heart, how He's revealed Himself in His Word and throughout history, who He says we are, how He calls us to live. We need to be able to withstand lies, to evaluate the claims of pastors and professors, to be like the Bereans who were "examining the Scriptures daily to see if these things were so" (Acts 17:11). We need to be like Mary who chose "the good portion"—to sit at Jesus' feet (Luke 10:38–42). This is my primary aim in part one of this book, to help you form biblical convictions about what it means to be a woman.

And when we are women of conviction, we will be so compelled by God's love for us in Jesus that we will live *coram Deo*— before His face. We will be women of courage—women who fear the Lord and not others, who can stand up under the onslaught of the enemy. We will know our own minds. We won't be swayed by claims that we must trade our womanhood to get dignity.[3] We won't be persuaded by those who tempt us to doubt God's heart toward us or his actions in history. We won't be willing to trade a lifetime of delight in our Savior for the promise of power here and now. We will be women who speak the truth, who advocate for the least of these, who live for a kingdom not of this world. We will be women who face the future without fearing for ourselves, or for our daughters. This is my goal for part two, to offer some field notes for feminine life in a challenging world. To instill courage.

As I write these words, I confess I feel a bit like I did that day: so convinced of God's heart toward women; so desperate to call you to believe it too. And also, like I just want to hide in the bathroom.

But I'm convinced this path through conviction toward courage is the call for God's daughters and those who love them, and I hope this book provides support, language, and hope for the days ahead. Though I have not figured out all the ins and outs of being a woman, I'm a woman raising women nonetheless. And I firmly believe the Bible teaches that there is a place for me, and there is a place for you. So I stand *coram Deo*, looking to the Scriptures for courage and clarity, and I offer this book to help point the way— for my daughters, and for you.

2

Wanted

ON RECOGNIZING YOUR VALUE

"I'll try to do and be anything you want me, if you'll only keep me."

ANNE SHIRLEY, *ANNE OF GREEN GABLES*

Matthew and Marilla Cuthbert wanted a boy. A boy could pull his weight, helping the brother and sister with farm chores as they aged. But instead, they got Anne Shirley. Not only was Anne decidedly *not* a boy, she was also everything they imagined a girl to be: scrawny and dramatic—a fountain of words, emotions, and imagination that puzzled the new foster parents. So, they determined, they had to take her back to the orphanage.

"You don't want me because I'm not a boy!" Anne lamented. "I might have expected it. Nobody ever did want me. I might have known it was all too beautiful to last. I might have known nobody really did want me."[1] Marilla rolled her eyes and maintained her resolve, but when the time came to return Anne, she couldn't bring herself to do it. The child could return to Green Gables and live with the Cuthberts, provided she would be on her best behavior. "I'll try to do and be anything you want me," Anne promises, "if you'll only keep me."[2]

Second-Class Status

Anne Shirley isn't the first little girl to try to prove she's worth keeping around, just as Matthew and Marilla aren't the only ones who dream of sons. Consider the historical record: Male heirs bring muscle to the family operation, guarantee a continued family line, and are born with the opportunity to bring honor to their parents as they pursue positions of influence in society. Daughters, however, have historically been considered a drain on family resources. They will cost the family a dowry or a wedding and then they will bear children in someone else's lineage.

We can't simply relegate these ideas to antiquity. Since 1941, US polls indicate that parents prefer sons.[3] One study reveals that parents invest more in their sons and brag about them more on social media.[4] And the two most populous countries in the world—India and China—have a history of gender-selective abortion and female infanticide that continues to this day.[5]

Throughout history, Christianity has provided a refuge for women, giving them a place of dignity, encouraging their education, and providing for discarded female infants, daughters, wives, and widows. In the Old Testament, the Levitical laws that seem strange and oppressive to us actually served to protect women, providing a stark contrast to the surrounding cultures of the ancient Near East. The New Testament documents women's unprecedented participation in Christ's ministry and that of the early church. "Within the Christian subculture women enjoyed far higher status than did women in the Greco-Roman world at large," writes historian Rodney Stark.[6]

Unfortunately, that doesn't mean Christian women aren't still acquainted with feeling unwanted, even among God's people. The beliefs and practices of our time and place (alongside the sin in our hearts) can cloud biblical interpretation and distort our application. Old Testament stories illustrate the Israelites' tendency to adopt the harmful practices of their neighbors, documenting polygamy, sexual assault, and abuse.[7]

And despite the New Testament's account of women's discipleship and partnership in ministry, much of early Christian teaching about the passages restricting women from particular offices or functions wrongly assume these limitations imply women have an inferior nature. Peter does refer to women as the "weaker vessel" (1 Peter 3:7), but I believe he has women's relatively weaker physical strength (and need for protection) in view. He's not affirming the Greco-Roman beliefs that women are the emotionally, spiritually, and morally inferior sex. We'll look at this in more depth in chapter 5.

The church has reflected the culture in many of its views and practices related to women over the years. Today, many sisters within the church attest to their perceived status, whether spoken or unspoken, of second-class, deceiver, usurper, seductress, or busybody. We're often viewed with suspicion, as if we're all gunning for the pastor or the pulpit.

These narratives worm their way into our hearts and we find ourselves inadvertently buying into the idea that women have less value. Maybe we wish for sons. Or we simply nod our heads as our friends lament their daughters' emotions or roll their eyes at "girl drama." At the very least, we feel in our bones that our womanhood is too much. That we are too much.

Maybe we feel misunderstood or too aggressive whenever we speak up in job interviews, political debates, theology discussions, and company meetings. Or maybe we don't speak up and feel ashamed of our silence. Maybe we experience misogyny and sexism firsthand and find ourselves among a community of women who are all too familiar with feeling unwanted or less than. Maybe we hear all the messages that come out of pulpits and Christian books, or maybe we just look in the mirror at a life that feels like it never measures up, and we begin to wonder. What are we worth?

How to Define Value

All of us—male and female—are inadvertently taught to measure our value in myriad ways across the span of ages and seasons. We look to our parents and peers for approval. We consume messages from all directions about the "right" way to look, feel, and behave. But there's something inherently feminine about this question of value, purpose, and place. The expectations for women pile into an unbearable burden. We're supposed to be soft but strong, successful but available, competent but not domineering, vulnerable but not weak, dependent but not needy, and the list goes on.

Apart from any intervening truth, we can end up looking back on an exhausting life spent trying desperately to prove we're good enough. It's no surprise that one of the most resonant movie lines in 2023 was this: "It is literally impossible to be a woman."[8]

DEFINING VALUE

Whether you've wrestled with your value as a woman or simply as a human, the fact is that we all want to believe we matter. But defining value is complicated. Consider our word choice. "Value" is an economic term. We use it to define something's usefulness or importance. And, deep down, that's often what we mean when we evaluate our own value and that of others. We frame it in terms of what someone has to offer.

Modern society prioritizes achievement and measures people in terms of their success, and we silently comply, grasping for meaningful ways to contribute. We want to know we're necessary, to feel like we belong. And so, to conjure these feelings, we hustle. We settle for the attention of a boy or a boss, social media likes and follows, the flawed belief that if people think we're awesome, that must mean we are. We esteem positions of power and resent the humble or hidden, often sacrificing more than we intend as we race toward some ever-moving finish line.

OVER-DEFINING WOMANHOOD

We're prone to adopt this economic definition of value within the church as well. We get specific about what it means to be a woman, making lists, drawing neat lines, and carving out a distinct space for feminine endeavors. But we define womanhood too narrowly, adding more than Scripture prescribes, and so we end up undermining the very value we're trying to affirm, because the resulting expectations just create another stage on which we can perform: Look at how we raise those babies, make that organic meal, or curate our bodies and spaces. We're like salespeople offering a unique value proposition: *Look at what I can do!* Pretty soon, we feel more like a dancing monkey, trying to win the praise of the crowds because our very identity is at stake. Those who don't fall within tidy categories are eyed with suspicion or excluded altogether. This leaves Christian women trying to prove we're the right kind of woman—the one who is truly valued.

In our striving, I wonder how many of us feel like the overlooked heroine who wonders if anyone will ever notice just how much she has to contribute. My family loves *Hamilton*, the

Broadway musical written by Lin-Manuel Miranda, and its final number gets me every time. The song echoes with a question: *Who will tell your story?* It considers how Alexander Hamilton is remembered by his peers, culminating in how his wife, Eliza, spent her years following his untimely death. As she lists accomplishment after accomplishment, desperately pleading for more time to carry on Alexander's legacy and to carve out her own, it suddenly dawns on us: It's this play! This is the story! And while it's certainly a play about Alexander, in many ways, it's really a play about Eliza. As the show closes, Eliza realizes it too. She looks up and finds the fourth wall removed, beholding a tear-filled audience that has just borne witness to her story.[9] Perhaps she has done enough.

BEING BEFORE DOING

As satisfying as it may be to think our lives have value if they conclude with a story to tell, there's another question in this closing number that haunts me: *When my time is up, have I done enough?* Eliza's harried list of accomplishments sounds a lot like our own. What if no one tells our story? When will we have done enough to prove we're worthy? At the end of the day, defining value in economic terms is incomplete at best. If we believe our value is defined only by what we do, we'll be plagued by envy and exhaustion. Someone will always do it better, and it's not clear who gets to declare the winner. After all our striving, we'll either despair about our inability to do enough, or we'll fall into a sort of wearying pride at our apparent ability to keep up. And once we achieve all that we've been working for? It will turn to dust in our fingers. Value we hustle for is value easily lost.

Nonetheless, it's not that crazy that we evaluate value through the lens of function. "Christianity—indeed, all ancient thought—is thoroughly *teleological*," Abigail Favale writes. "The 'whatness' of a thing, its essential identity, is connected to its purpose."[10] David VanDrunen agrees, writing, "What human beings were made to be and what they were made to do cannot be separated."[11] God created Adam and Eve with dignity and value, *and* he gave them work to do. Ever since the Garden, each of us is born with an intrinsic desire to know the end for which we're created, rightly seeing a straight line between our *being* and our *doing*. We'll get to the *doing*, but we need to start by recognizing our problem with the order and emphasis. *Being* ought to precede *doing*, but we tend to want to jump over our *being* and fixate on our *doing*, letting our performance have the final say on who we are.

Instead, we need to look at value on God's terms, as human beings broadly and as women specifically. As created beings, our value is received, not earned. It must be defined outside of us. That means it's not about what we contribute, it's about who made us and why. We must see ourselves as those created by God, formed in His image, crafted to be women, and redeemed by His Son. This is the narrative that defines our value—unchanging and outside of us—and it's the foundational conviction we must form before we can go any further.

Notes on Biblical Interpretation

I grew up believing the Bible was merely a collection of stories and rules. Basically, the stories illustrated the rules. The Scriptures told me how to be good—how to get saved, and how to stay saved. There was no beauty there, only a relentless God who was always disappointed in me. That's the God and Bible I abandoned in college.

A few years later, a friend gifted my two-year-old daughter *The Jesus Storybook Bible* by Sally Lloyd-Jones. I was irritated. We weren't attending church at the time, and I had made up my mind that I would protect my daughter from God. But Hadley loved the book and begged me to read it to her every night. And, every night, I held back tears as I read the stories I had always known reimagined to illuminate their ultimate purpose—to point to God's redemptive work throughout history culminating in His Son. Sally Lloyd-Jones taught me how to read the Bible. She writes,

> *The Bible isn't mainly about me and what I should be doing. It's about God and what he has done. . . . The Bible is most of all a story—the story of how God loves his children and comes to rescue them. . . . In spite of everything, no matter what, whatever it cost him—God won't ever stop loving his children . . . with a wonderful, Never Stopping, Never Giving Up, Unbreaking, Always and Forever Love. . . . The Bible, in short, is a Story—not a Rule Book—and there is only one Hero in the Story.[12]*

One of my primary goals in these first few chapters is to reframe how we approach the Scriptures, especially Genesis 1–3. We have worn out these pages of our Bibles trying to figure out what they say about what it means to be human and what it means to be female. It makes sense—they are our origin story, the Bible's explanation for how it all began and how it's going. That also means it makes sense that these chapters and their interpretation are some of the most disputed in Scripture.

I don't want to downplay their difficulty, but I do want to challenge the way we approach these difficult texts. When we come to the Bible demanding it answers the questions we pose, we risk becoming reductionistic and anachronistic. We focus on squeezing out lessons for our lives here and now and neglect the passage's aim for its first audience, written in a particular time and place. And, in so doing, we miss the invitation to freedom and abundance embedded in its ultimate goal—the revelation of Christ.

All of Scripture is profitable for us in many ways (2 Tim. 3:16). There are lessons for us to learn, definitions and instructions for how we're to live our lives. True biblical conviction will move us to grateful obedience. But we must let the text speak on its own terms.[13] It will answer our questions, though often not in the ways we hope.

Crafted by God

Moses, the author of Genesis, writes the story of creation in two scenes, each offering a different perspective. First, he zooms out and gives us the big picture. The broader creation narrative of chapter 1 demonstrates the dignity and value of humankind broadly, male and female. We'll get to the unique value of God's female image bearers, but the Scriptures start with what is shared and we do well to do the same.

In fact, it's worth noting that the Bible starts with God, not us. This is important. Though God welcomes our questions, our experiences of injustice, our pleading for fairness, we must start with Him. The question of a woman's value is first and foremost a theological one.[14]

In the beginning, it's just God, and He creates the heavens and the earth (Gen. 1:1). There's a striking contrast in the Bible's creation narrative compared to others of its time. Ancient mythology describes gods who create humans to do their bidding. They need

GOD CREATES NOT BECAUSE HE NEEDS TO, BUT BECAUSE HE WANTS TO. WE'RE CRAFTED BY THE GOD OF THE UNIVERSE OUT OF HIS SHEER DELIGHT!

servants—people to keep things in order so the gods can have their fun. Humans make up for their lack. But it's not so with the God of the Bible. Before time began, God exists in perfect Trinitarian love, Father, Son, and Holy Spirit. He is independent—He doesn't need anything outside of Himself. That means when He creates, He doesn't do so out of a deficiency. He creates not because He needs to, but because He wants to. This fact alone imbues creation with incredible value—we're crafted by the God of the universe out of His sheer delight!

We've seen how we tend to confuse being wanted with feeling needed, to jump over *being* to *doing*, to prove our value by how well we fulfill what God has created us for. But that's not the framework God establishes for us. God does create humanity for a purpose, but He blesses them first and *then* He gives them work to do (Gen. 1:28). Even with the task before them, He declares them "very good"—"not only partly good or as a means to an end, but simply as and for what [they are]"[15]—before they have done anything (Gen. 1:31). This is the first foundational piece of recognizing our value. You're valuable because God made you, and not simply because God made you, but because He *wanted* to make you.

Crafted In His Image

God also creates humanity *imago Dei*: in His image and likeness (Gen. 1:26–27). There are many facets to what it means to bear God's image.[16] Theologian Herman Bavinck summarizes it like this:

> *The whole person is the image of the whole, that is, the triune, God. The human soul, all human faculties, the virtues of knowledge, righteousness, and holiness, and even the human body images God.*[17]

We reflect God in all our human attributes and capabilities, in our "psychic capacities," and our "activities." . . . "The very diversity and abundance of these forces reflect God."[18] This is truly all-encompassing, and it's where we start to see the line between *being* and *doing*. We are created for a purpose, and that purpose is to image God. The *imago Dei* is what we are, and it's also what we do. In fact, perhaps the greater emphasis in the creation account is the vocational aspect of being created in God's image. He places Adam and Eve in the garden as His vice-rulers—He entrusts both of them to be partners in the task of ruling and representing Him, spreading His glory to the ends of the earth.[19]

We'll look more at how our image-bearing is reflected in our differentiated sexes in later chapters, and we'll consider how our image-bearing plays out after the fall (in chapter 3), and how it gives shape to our vocations (in chapter 4). But for now, I'd like to emphasize dignity. Humanity is bestowed with unique value, unlike any other created thing. We image God in our very being. The apostle James points to this reality when he condemns the church for using their tongues to tear each other down: "With [our tongue] we bless our Lord and Father, and with it we curse people who are made in the likeness of God. . . . My brothers, these things ought not to be so" (James 3:9–10). Our value is an unshakable reality, rooted in the God who made us, and it requires that we see and affirm the dignity of all image bearers, male and female.

I'd also like to observe here that our image-bearing is communal. Richard Phillips writes, "Just as God himself exists within loving community—Father, Son, and Spirit experiencing eternal and perfect love—mankind bears God's image in relationships of community and love."[20] It's not only valuable for men and women to live in community together for their mutual flourishing, it's also a way that we image God together. In community, we reflect

God's loving Trinitarian relationship, but we also reflect Him in our complementary relationships with one another. Our differences—not only as men and woman, but as different humans with varied personalities, experiences, ethnic backgrounds, interests, and gifts—image a God of abundant creativity and love.

Crafted to be Female

To recap: The basis for our value is unchanging. We have value because we're created by an independent, Trinitarian God of love who chose to make us out of sheer delight. We have value because we're created in His image, made to reflect and represent Him in every aspect of our being and doing. This is true of all human beings, male and female.

But now I want to wrestle with the question I posed at the start of the chapter—what about *girls*? What unique value do they have? What is distinct and beautiful and good about being crafted by God to be female?

Thus far, we've focused on Moses' broader telling of the creation story in Genesis 1. This version emphasizes Adam and Eve's equality and unity. They're treated as a unit—humankind—and what is true for one is true for the other. As male and female, they are created in God's image, share equal dignity and value, and receive God's blessing and commission.

The difficulty comes when the story zooms in. God creates Adam first, the Bible shows us (Gen. 2:7). Eve comes later and, if we're honest, sometimes we wonder if she's an afterthought. It's as if God realized Adam would need a "little helper"—someone to boost his ego, bear his children, and do his laundry. Later, it appears Eve led Adam astray, and the misogynist narrative begins: Wouldn't the human race have been better off without her? Doesn't her second-born-deceiver status label her as someone to be ruled, a reckless force to be tamed? Certainly, it seems like her only real contribution is babies. No wonder we're hustling to prove we deserve to be here. People throughout history have used the creation narrative to justify these perspectives, and we'll look more closely at their arguments.

But what if we're missing something?

It should go without saying, but Moses intentionally places Genesis 1 before Genesis 2. Some scholars try to reconcile the difficulty of a second creation account by arguing it was inserted by a different author. But, like many other places in Scripture, the two different views on the same event make different theological points. And the order matters. The first account—the big picture—establishes some essential, foundational truths, some of which we've already named: God's sovereign rule over creation, His independence, His Trinitarian love; the creation of mankind in God's image, their unity, blessedness, and calling.

We're not meant to set any of these truths aside as we venture into Genesis 2. Rather, what follows builds on what's already established. There are two things this narrative highlights that will help us form conviction about our value as females: First, the equality of the sexes alongside their distinction; second, the importance of the created order.

Equality Alongside Distinction

We live in an age where people have difficulty holding ideas in tension. On one side, you have those who argue the Bible only paints a picture of the equality of the sexes and any differentiation is culturally (and sinfully) imposed. Others see only distinction, over-defining the differences between men and women and pointing to biblical and historical caricatures to argue for clearcut divisions between male and female roles.

But the Bible doesn't cower to our human limitations. Rather, it invites us to a fuller vision for a flourishing humanity, where both equality and distinction are not in conflict with one another but rather are recognized and celebrated. Men and women can be equal while also given different roles to fulfill.

Genesis 1 has already established Adam and Eve's equality as image bearers, and it's beautifully reinforced in the up close account of Eve's creation in Genesis 2. After a thorough review of all other creatures, Adam finds no one suitable to be his companion (Gen. 2:19–20). But when he encounters Eve, it's as if he's bursting at the seams: "This at last is bone of my bones and flesh of my flesh; she shall be called Woman, because she was taken out of Man" (Gen. 2:23). The point here is their similarity to one another.[21] *She's like me!* Adam declares. He recognizes the woman as his equal, asserting her value and marveling at God's provision of her. This sameness is so pronounced in the text that Henri Blocher writes,

> *"Male and female" will never be anything more than a second truth about man and woman. History shows an ever-recurring tendency to imprison woman in her femininity to the detriment of her participating quite simply in human life. By underlining the likeness, Genesis provides protection against the coarse machismo of the Mediterranean male, but also against the suspect cult of an Eternal Feminine, and against Romantic speculations which make the masculine and the feminine, like yin and yang, the ultimate principles, the two poles of being.[22]*

Isn't that lovely? Our sex is an important truth about us. But it's the second truth.

WE NEED EACH OTHER

This second truth comes out as the account that celebrates equality also highlights difference. God creates Eve just as personally and intentionally as He does Adam. But there's a small difference: Instead of forming a new human from the dust as He did Adam, He pulls a bone from Adam's side. Puritan Matthew Henry famously observes God's lesson in this action: "The woman was made of a rib out of the side of Adam; not made out of his head to rule over him, nor out of his feet to be trampled upon by him, but out of his side to be equal with him, under his arm to be protected, and near his heart to be beloved."[23] The point here is complementarity. The term *complementarian* has a lot of baggage, and people hold diverse views under the complementarian label. But I think it's helpful language when we consider its definition, rather than its varied application today. Basically, the term means that, while both males and females are of equal value in God's creation, they have different roles to fulfill.

Men and women are created to complement—or complete—one another.

While Genesis 1 reveals God as independent, Genesis 2 shows man is not. God has no need for us; He just wants us. But Adam isn't God. Though he shares God's relational nature, existing as a solo act leaves something amiss.

IN DELAYING WOMAN'S CREATION, GOD LEFT SPACE FOR THE NARRATIVE TO EXPOSE OUR NEED FOR ONE ANOTHER.

After the repeated refrain throughout creation, "It was good," we're halted by the words, "not good": "Then the LORD God said, 'It is *not good* that the man should be alone'" (Gen. 2:18). Adam needs Eve.

Isn't it interesting that God establishes this reality before the fall? God creates man and then highlights a deficiency to make an important point: It's not sinful to need one another; it's human. We're not created to do life alone (Gen. 2:18).[24] Men need women; women need men (1 Cor. 11:11–12). Women were not an afterthought; we know from Genesis 1 that creation wasn't complete and declared "very good" until both man and woman were on the scene. But in delaying woman's creation, God left space for the narrative to expose our need for one another. Adam needed Eve, not to do his laundry, but to be his companion—a "helper fit for him" (Gen. 2:18).

EZER

This word "helper" has been giving women a headache for years, and I understand why. I've never enjoyed sharing the kitchen with my children. God has endowed many a woman with supernatural capacity to be surrounded by "mommy's helpers," but I've never been one of them. I value efficiency far too much to have to fish eggshells out of cake batter. At one point in the toddler years, I started setting up a station in the far corner of the kitchen, giving my kiddo some measuring cups and spoons, and letting them go wild with flour and a few eggs while I quickly whipped up whatever "we" were making. On a good day, they would be covered in flour while remaining none the wiser that they never actually contributed to the cookies that appeared in the oven.[25] It's easy to read "helper" and picture my toddlers stirring together meaningless ingredients, their backs to the real action. We might picture a little pat on the head, a "Thanks for contributing! What a good helper you are!" while we look at our useless bowls, wondering why we bothered.

WANTED

But this picture doesn't capture the Bible's intent. *Ezer*, translated "helper," is a word most often used throughout Scripture for the help God Himself provides.

"But I am poor and needy; hasten to me, O God!" the psalmist cries. "You are my help [*ezer*] and my deliverer; O Lord do not delay!" (Ps. 70:5).

Other psalms consider the help God provides, recalling His strength, mercy, and faithfulness: "I lift up my eyes to the hills. From where does my help [*ezer*] come from? My help [*ezer*] comes from the Lord, who made heaven and earth" (Ps. 121:1–2).

"Blessed is he whose help [*ezer*] is the God of Jacob, whose hope is in the Lord his God" (Ps. 146:5).

In the New Testament, when Jesus speaks of the promised Holy Spirit, Bible translators use the same word for Him: "And I will ask the Father, and he will give you another Helper, to be with you forever" (John 14:16).

Calling the woman a "helper fit" for Adam will help us when we consider the ways men and women are to labor alongside one another in chapter 4. God gives Eve to Adam to be an essential partner in the tasks of ruling, subduing, and filling the earth, as we'll see. He needs her contribution and perspective. But let's focus for a minute on what this says about the woman's *being*. Her very *presence* is necessary. This zoomed-in story shows us the value of community as men and women live alongside one another, existing together in complementary ways. Because both are created in God's image, each has an intrinsic dignity and value on their own, but here the Bible asserts the distinct value of men and women together, showing they are both crucial for the flourishing of humanity.

Created Order Matters

Have you noticed how I've deftly avoided any discussion of roles up to this point? In part, that's because we'll do a deep dive into a woman's vocation in later chapters, and considering the different roles of men and women fits better there. But it's also because we need to establish men and women's equal dignity and value as those created by God and formed in His image first. We need to see woman's unique value and God's goodness in creating us female. And now we need to turn to an important topic that, if treated wrongly, threatens to undermine a woman's value: headship. It's time to talk about why the woman was created second.

"Headship" is up there with "helper" in the list of biblical terms that cause women problems. But headship brings some baggage of its own, in part because the word itself isn't in the chapters we've been reviewing. This is a case where the creation narrative shows instead of tells, and the room that leaves for interpretation is a bit dicey.

THE APOSTLE PAUL CLAIMS THERE'S SOMETHING TO THE FACT THAT GOD CREATED ADAM FIRST.

When we talk about male headship, we generally have in mind the complementarian belief that the Bible reserves the roles of head of household and pastor/elder for men only. This belief is rooted in New Testament passages, where the apostles outline very specific contexts in which men hold authority over women. Some would apply this more broadly, as in all men are the head of all women. (They're wrong.) Rather, a wife is to submit to her own husband (1 Cor. 11:3; Eph. 5:22), and all laypeople, men and women, are to submit to their elders (Heb. 13:17), who are to be qualified men (1 Tim. 2:12; 3:1–7). We'll look more closely at Paul's words about headship and submission in the next couple of chapters. What I want you to see right now is the way Paul points back to the created order in Genesis as the foundation for his teaching about how headship plays out in Christian homes and churches. He claims there's something to the fact that God created Adam first.

There are people who want to tell you that Paul is a product of his time, or that he's misinterpreting Scripture here. The created order doesn't matter, they say; this is just a superfluous detail and Genesis emphasizes equality and unity for this first couple. The problem, though, is that the Bible doesn't agree. Genesis does give us a picture of men and women created equal in dignity and value. But they are also distinct. So, does the New Testament's teaching about the created order cast a shadow on the case for feminine value?

THE ROYAL COMMISSION

To answer that, we have to zoom back out and review the Genesis narrative again. This time, instead of looking at Genesis as the foundation of "male and female he created them" (Gen. 1:27), we need to remember that these first chapters are also the foundation of the Bible, the starting point for the story of God's redemption of all things in Christ.[26] And part of that foundation-laying is establishing God's

THE TREE OF THE KNOWLEDGE OF GOOD AND EVIL PROVIDES A TESTING GROUND WHERE ADAM STANDS AS THE REPRESENTATIVE OF THE WHOLE HUMAN RACE.

covenantal nature. Covenants provide the structure for God's dealings with His people and for Scripture.[27] In Genesis 1–2, God reveals Himself as the great King who is ruler over His people. By placing His image on humanity, He enters into a covenant with them, commissioning them for an important task—to spread His glory to the ends of the earth. If they succeed, they will gain eternal life with God.[28]

By creating Adam first, God establishes Adam as the representative of the whole human race, a theological concept known as federal headship. As federal head, Adam's obedience or disobedience will be credited to everyone who comes after him. He can earn eternal life—or death—for himself and his posterity.

The New Testament explains the concept of federal headship (see Rom. 5:12, 18–19 below), but we can also see it in how Moses structures this second creation account. Both Adam and Eve receive instructions in Genesis 1:28, to "Be fruitful and multiply and fill the earth and subdue it, and have dominion over the fish of the sea and over the birds of the heavens and over every living thing that moves on the earth." But in Genesis 2, God gives Adam additional instructions. He entrusts him with the royal commission to protect and keep the garden (Gen. 2:15) and warns him not to eat from the tree of the knowledge of good and evil (Gen. 2:16–17). We'll consider these instructions a bit later, but notice here that the tree provides a testing ground for Adam, setting the stage for what will happen in the fall.

The whole point of the text is to put Adam's obedience on display.[29] Will he keep God's covenant? The narrative is artfully written, with an arc meant to build tension until we arrive at the fateful climax—the moment Adam takes a bite—marked by one Hebrew word that means "and he ate" (Gen. 3:6)

SETTING THE STAGE FOR REDEMPTION

The truth is, from a literary perspective, Eve is secondary to this narrative. Adam is the main player. It would be understandable if this bothered you a bit. As Americans living in an individualistic age, we wonder why we can't just represent ourselves. And as women, we wonder why we need a man to stand in our place. Why couldn't God just give Adam and Eve their own covenants, each one striving to make it to the top?

But the point in displaying Adam as the main player and emphasizing his obedience to God's covenant is not about his maleness, superiority, or power. It's not meant to somehow diminish the value or role of women; it's to set the stage for God's unfolding plan of redemption. Adam has a particular role in redemptive history. As the head of humanity, he can achieve eternal life for himself and all humanity by keeping God's covenant. This also means that, though Eve is deceived, Adam is the one held accountable— the one through whom sin enters the world (Gen. 3:6; Rom. 5:12; 1 Tim. 2:14). All of this points forward to Christ. Messing with the created order messes with the gospel. We all need a Man to stand in our place! Thank God for the Second Adam!

Therefore, just as sin came into the world through one man, and death through sin, and so death spread to all men because all sinned. . . . Therefore, as one trespass led to condemnation for all men, so one act of righteousness leads to justification and life for all men. For as by the one man's disobedience the many were made sinners, so by the one man's obedience the many will be made righteous. (Rom. 5:12, 18–19)

When we view these chapters through a redemptive-historical lens, it lifts our eyes to Christ as we see God's beautiful purpose for headship from the beginning, to establish a means for providing eternal life for His image bearers.

There is much more to say about what this all means—what headship looks like today, how men and women uniquely complement each other, what happens when it all goes wrong. There's time to get to all that. But don't miss this: The point of the created order is not to communicate that we're God's second choice, it's to communicate the nature of our salvation. The importance of the created order can be true alongside the testimony of the whole creation narrative, which affirms our value not just as humans but as women.

Redeemed by Jesus

So, what about sin?

The difficulty in sticking with the beautiful, created ideal of Genesis 1–2 is that we know what happens when we turn the pages of our Bibles. It wasn't enough for our first parents to bear God's image; they wanted to be gods themselves (Gen. 3:5–6). And every one of us since is born into sin that distorts God's image and tries to undermine our worth by our treasonous works. Our enemy calls our value into question, accusing us night and day (Rev. 12:10). The shame within our own consciences follows us around, tempting us to doubt our place before God and others.

We'll spend the rest of this book looking at the impact of sin on our womanhood and our relationships, wrestling through what it means to be female in a fallen world.

But even in our sinful state, our value stands. As redemption unfolds, God asserts the final say: These creatures made in His image are worth saving. We are so valuable, and he loves us so deeply, that He will send His one and only Son to save us (John 3:16). "You were bought with a price," the apostles write, "not with perishable things such as silver or gold, but with the precious blood of Christ" (1 Cor. 6:20; 1 Peter 1:18–19).

So while we ought not to curse those made in God's image, how much more should we esteem those for whom Christ died? (See Rom. 14:15; 1 Cor. 8:11; Gal. 6:10.) Christ has settled our value, paying the penalty our sin deserves and giving us His righteousness. There's no condemnation left for us in Him (Rom. 8:1, 33–34). Though God's image is distorted in us because of sin, in Christ and by His Spirit, we have been given a "new self, which is being renewed in knowledge after the image of its creator" (Col. 3:10). As redeemed image bearers, our maleness and femaleness become all the more beautiful as we learn to live together in a way that pictures Christ and His church, a flourishing household that continues to reflect the beauty and diversity of the Godhead.

Your Value Is . . . Simply Received

In this chapter, I set out to lay the foundation for what follows. We have questions about the place for women in the church, home, and society. These are very real issues we need to address. Misogyny and sexism are alive and well in many spaces.

But first we need to answer the question beneath those questions: *What is the value of a woman? Does she matter?*

And, perhaps, the question beneath those questions: *Do I matter? What is* my *value?*

I've argued that the answer to this question is first and foremost theological. Feeling unwanted and undervalued are practically universal female experiences, but our value is nonetheless unshakable because it's defined outside of us. The God of the universe created us out of His sheer delight, crafted us in His image, and redeemed us by the blood of His Son. He gets the final say about our worth.

I've also argued that we're not just generically valuable as humans; we're specifically valuable as women. God intentionally created two complementary sexes for their mutual joy and partnership. We'll spend the rest of the book fleshing out what that looks like, but for now, the point is this: Our value is fixed and outside of us. It isn't something we can hustle for, and it's not lessened by being born female. It's simply received.

If we don't believe this, we'll find ourselves echoing Anne Shirley with promises to prove ourselves. We'll skip over the *being* and get on to the *doing*, jumping into the hamster wheel of life as a performer. But if you've spent any time with Anne Shirley through L. M. Montgomery's books, you know she didn't exactly live up to her promise to "do and be anything" the Cuthberts wanted her to be. She couldn't help herself. She was constantly in her own way, unable to be the useful and well-behaved orphan the Cuthberts were hoping for.

But it turns out that was the point. What made Anne so delightful was not her *doing* but her *being*. She never needed to prove her value after all; it was there all along. The drama, the words, the emotions, the imagination—in all these ways and more—Anne turned out to be exactly what the Cuthberts needed. Her presence was the gift. And so is yours.

3

Storied

ON BEING DEFINED BY MERCY

Jesus stood up and said to her, "Woman, where are they? Has no one condemned you?" She said, "No one, Lord." And Jesus said, "Neither do I condemn you; go, and from now on sin no more."

JOHN 8:10–11

I've always been drawn to stories where women stepped outside their expected roles. As a kid, we rented movies every Friday night. With seven in my family, seven movies for seven dollars meant not only an incredible steal but also the elimination of any squabbles as we each raced through Blockbuster to make our selections. (Remember Blockbuster??)

Most weeks, I would march to the familiar shelf and pick up the same battered copy of *A League of Their Own*. I'm not sure how long my streak lasted before my mom finally put her foot down (and bought me my very own VHS copy of the movie), but my admiration for Dottie Hinson, the movie's fictional baseball star in the All-American Girls Professional Baseball League, lived on. I even tried to defy my lack of baseball skills and form my own girls baseball team, which, admittedly, only ever had four players and one anticlimactic practice.

Strength and Courage

It wasn't just sports movies, though *Little Giants* remains a family favorite; it was any story where the woman showed her strength and courage, her willingness to defy stereotypes and rise above the rules trying to keep her down—movies like *Wild Hearts Can't Be Broken* and *Mona Lisa Smile*. I longed to be the heroine, not the damsel in distress, which probably explains my tomboyish childhood leanings and my always-dirty feet, the result of summers spent running barefoot through the neighborhood, building forts and climbing trees. I imagined myself a brave adventurer, an explorer, a rebel, or perhaps a CIA agent á la Sydney Bristow of *Alias*.

I admired the other more bookish protagonists too. Spending hours curled up with a book under the lilac bush in our backyard, I pretended I was Anne Shirley or Jo March. I relished being the smart kid, and even while I worked hard to beat the boys in my class at foot races and recess sports, I particularly enjoyed winning at essays and spelling tests.

Deep down, though, I also pined to be wanted, dreaming of the day I'd finally be caught up in my own love story. I loved when shows featured makeovers and imagined the moment when that boy I beat would finally look up and realize I was smart and fast *and* beautiful.

Fallen Womanhood

Stories have this way of shaping us, of getting into our bodies and souls, forming our identities and values. We may not even notice that, over time, they become the stories we tell ourselves about how the world works, about who we are in it. And when it comes to womanhood, there are a plethora of stories out there, ones that inspire, and others that shame. And there is a true and beautiful one that re-stories us, rightly placing us before the Author Himself.

GENESIS 3 MARKS A TURNING POINT THAT SETS THE TRAJECTORY FOR THE REST OF HUMAN HISTORY.

EVE: VILLAIN OR HEROINE?

The Bible paints a portrait of the inherent dignity and value of God's image bearers, male and female. As the creation narrative ends, the king and queen are enthroned, ready to serve side by side in God's garden. All is well in the world. But when we turn the page to Genesis 3 and zoom in on the female prototype, we find the ignition point for many a modern fire.[1] Our mother Eve is used in countless lessons to warn of our so-called propensities as women—to be deceived, to usurp, to covet, to fall (and lead) into temptation. We know little of Eve's virtues, so we're mostly warned of her vices. Womanhood is dripping with power we must learn to suppress, the story goes, or we might take the human race down with us.

Genesis 3 marks a turning point that sets the trajectory for the rest of human history. We're caught up in a story, but suddenly the characters are dark and shadowy, and we are among them. We find ourselves on unfamiliar paths, our womanhood a liability. Is Eve the villain or the heroine? And what does that say about us? Doesn't our fall into sin call our value into question?

We do have to face the reality of sin and its consequences. We must not shy away from its implications for our womanhood. But we also must form biblical conviction here, or we'll be swept up in a story that's neither true nor good but holds power over us nonetheless.

We need to start with the story as it unfolds in Scripture. A villain, the serpent, enters the scene and approaches the woman (Gen. 3:1). We can't say for sure why the serpent approached Eve instead of Adam. We've already discussed the importance of the created order, and what some scholars see here is an intentional subversion of God's design, tempting Adam to shirk his headship duties, or tempting Eve to usurp authority that isn't hers. But I think it's more compelling to see the way the narrative artfully demonstrates creation's ordering, disordering, and reordering rather than making a statement about Adam's exercise of headship.[2] What we can say for sure is that Eve finds the serpent's proposition compelling. She assesses the fruit, determines God has withheld from her, and invites her husband, "who was with her" (Gen. 3:6), to join in partaking.

HOW FAR THEY HAVE FALLEN

The consequences are catastrophic. In just seven verses, the newlyweds have gone from being naked and not ashamed (Gen. 2:25) to being aware of their nakedness and desperately trying to cover and hide (Gen. 3:7–8). They immediately experience shame and fracturing within their relationship as a result of sin entering the world. Their delight in God's presence is replaced by fear (Gen. 3:10). When God calls out to Adam and confronts his actions, Adam responds by throwing his bride under the bus, even calling into question God's goodness in giving him this wife: "The woman whom you gave to be with me, she gave me fruit of the tree, and I ate" (Gen. 3:12). Eve also shifts the blame, pointing out the serpent's deception (Gen. 3:13).

What follows is God's pronouncement of judgment, first on

the serpent, then the woman, then the man (Gen. 3:14–19), and as we reach the end of the story and see the man and woman cast out of the garden, our heads hang low with them. How far they have fallen from their created ideal! How desperately we feel the weight of their sin and ours, of its consequences throughout the generations.

Two Competing Stories

It's no wonder this story has conjured numerous interpretations as we try to make sense of our lives in a fallen world. From the pivotal moments arise questions that are painful to ask and difficult to answer. "The serpent deceived me, and I ate," Eve tells God (Gen. 3:13), and perhaps we wonder if the serpent approached Eve because she was the weak link. What are we to make of female propensities given Eve's status as the one deceived? Is she gullible? Unable to be trusted? Easily led astray?

We also don't know what to make of Eve's judgment: "To the woman he said, 'I will surely multiply your pain in childbearing; in pain you shall bring forth children. Your desire shall be for your husband, and he shall rule over you.'" (Gen. 3:16).[3] Is this the foundation of the battle of the sexes? The beginning of male domination and the exploitation of women? Does it mean women are inherent usurpers, or that men are inherent abusers? And what do our experiences of life post-Eden mean for how we're to understand not only this passage, but also God's heart for His fallen image bearers? Two primary stories compete to offer answers to these questions.

ARE WOMEN THE PROBLEM?

One side tells us that women are the problem. Interpreting the apostle Paul's prohibition on women teachers, for example, church father Chrysostom summarizes the view shared by many throughout history: "The woman taught once, and ruined all. On this account therefore he says, let her not teach. But what is it to other women, that she suffered this? It certainly concerns them; for the sex is weak and fickle, and he is speaking of the sex collectively."[4] Tertullian's language is even more condemning:

> *And do you not know that you are (each) an Eve? The*
> *sentence of God on this sex of yours lives in this age: the guilt*
> *must of necessity live too. You are the devil's gateway: you are*
> *the unsealer of that (forbidden) tree: you are the first deserter*
> *of the divine law: you are she who persuaded him whom*
> *the devil was not valiant enough to attack. You destroyed so*
> *easily God's image, man. On account of your desert—that is,*
> *death—even the Son of God had to die.*[5]

Some see the weakness of the female sex as part of Eve's created design, others see it as punishment for her sin, and many tellers of this story argue from their experiences with gullible women, Jezebels, busybodies, and usurpers. In this story, the abrasive and rebellious feminist movement of the last century provide even more evidence indicting women. This story shames Eve's daughters as it demands that we know our place and submit to the men in our lives as a necessary protection against our own sinful proclivities.

OR HAS IT ALWAYS BEEN MEN?

Another story counters, arguing the problem has always been the men. A recent *New York Times* bestseller begins with "A Brief History of the Patriarchy." The patriarchy, Elise Loehnen writes, "has defined Western culture for millennia. Its forefathers

STORIED

adopted and shaped early Christianity to enforce behavior in ways that continue to affect us."[6] Beth Allison Barr starts her book *The Making of Biblical Womanhood* in a similar vein. She considers the church's teaching on male headship alongside factors like unequal pay, disdain for "women's work," and a history of women's oppression in the church and broader culture, and she concludes, "Rather than being different from the world, Christians [are] just like everyone else in their treatment of women."[7]

This narrative explains away the previous one, pointing to a room full of men who pull the puppet strings, doing everything they can to preserve their power. It's men who define the standards for women, and they are oppressive and demeaning. Loehnen writes, "What exactly constitutes a good woman? The patriarchal paradigm of femininity—selfless, physically perfect, nurturing, obedient, compliant, modest, responsible, self-effacing—persists. Women are expected to 'know their place'—firmly outside, yet supporting circles of power—and abide by it."[8] The patriarchy exists to keep women down, this story goes, and we must work to expose its roots and rewrite the narrative in a way that honors and elevates women.

MISSING THE BEAUTIFUL STORY

If you've ever examined either of these narratives closely, I imagine you've found that the former chafes, but the latter beckons. We resent labels that peg us as the cause of society's ills, and we know all too well the reality of misogyny, sexism, being underestimated, or excluded on the basis of sex. But the truth is that both stories can make compelling arguments, and neither gets the whole thing wrong. And both miss the more beautiful story that I believe the Bible gives us, starting right there with a disgraced Eve in the garden. There are good answers to the questions we've posed, found outside of the narratives fighting to persuade us to doubt God's goodness. The Bible's answers invite us into a beautiful womanhood lived in view of God's mercies. But to get there, we have to give the story another pass, willing to hold our preconceived ideas loosely as we examine our biblical roots.

Why Was Eve Deceived?

One of the first principles of Bible interpretation is that Scripture interprets Scripture. We've already practiced this in the last chapter as we considered the New Testament's commentary on Genesis 1–3. We'll continue that here, looking specifically at Paul's words in 1 Timothy and his interpretation of what happened in the fall. Using Genesis to support his point that the office of pastor/elder is reserved for qualified men (1 Tim. 3:1–7), Paul says, "I do not permit a woman to teach or to exercise authority over a man; rather, she is to remain quiet. For Adam was formed first, then Eve; and Adam was not deceived, but the woman was deceived and became a transgressor" (1 Tim. 2:12–14).[9]

At face value, and as Chrysostom argues, it appears Paul is drawing a straight line from two points on Eve's story—from her second-created status and her deception to restrictions on her teaching or holding authority over men.[10] If you see women as the problem, this confirms some kind of inherent deficiency in the female sex, grounding the argument that women are emotionally, intellectually, and spiritually inferior to men. If you see men as the problem, this text is just a testimony to the patriarchy's sinister role in casting women as villains in order to justify their exercise of power and oppression. (I should add: I'm intentionally representing two extremes here. To be fair, there are egalitarian interpretations of this passage that don't dismiss the Bible as a product of the patriarchy. And there are complementarian arguments that are more moderate in their understanding of what Paul is saying about women.)

But I'm not satisfied with either of these explanations and, I hope, neither are you.

DOES SCRIPTURE SAY WOMEN ARE DEFICIENT?

To help us wade through these stories, another principle of biblical interpretation is helpful: Since we believe Scripture doesn't contradict itself, we can use the clear passages of the Bible to help us understand texts that are difficult.[11]

So, what is the apostle Paul implying in 1 Timothy? Does he mean God created Eve—and all women—with an inferior nature?

This should be an easy one to refute from the rest of Scripture. We saw that both Adam and Eve are created in God's image (Gen. 1:26–28), and with that comes equal dignity and value. But also, God's creation is *good. Very good,* in fact (Gen. 1:31). If God created Eve with a deficiency, making her morally, spiritually, intellectually, and emotionally inferior to men, wouldn't this be a defect in God's creation? And wouldn't Adam be just to accuse God of malpractice in giving him a flawed partner (Gen. 3:12)?

Instead, God calls Eve a helper fit for Adam (Gen. 2:18). He places her at Adam's side, showing they each have an important part to play in carrying out their mission. To understand that, we need to dig deeper into the vocational aspect of image-bearing that I mentioned in chapter 2, and show how it contradicts claims about a deficient female nature. Our creation in God's image settles humanity's value, but it also gives us a job to do. G. K. Beale writes, "Just as God, after his initial work of creation subdued the chaos, ruled over it, and further created and filled the earth with all kinds of animate life, so Adam and Eve, in their garden abode, were to reflect God's activities in Genesis 1 by fulfilling the commission to 'subdue' and 'rule over all the earth' and to 'be fruitful and multiply.'"[12]

CREATED TO BE PROPHETS, PRIESTS, KINGS

This is the essence of what it means to be made in God's image, to reflect God's "divine attributes" and his "functions," as Benjamin Gladd writes.[13] Theologians often describe these functions in terms of offices—prophet, priest, and king. As prophets, Adam and Eve receive God's word and are responsible to understand, obey, and teach it to those who come after them.[14] Further, God's garden is also His sanctuary, and placed there as priests, Adam and Eve are "fashioned to mediate God's presence and to worship and serve before him."[15] And as kings, Adam and Eve subdue God's creation, extending God's rule to the ends of the earth.

Adam had been charged with the task of working and keeping the garden (Gen. 2:15). This language—to work and keep— is the same language given to the Levite priests for their work at the tabernacle, and later, the temple.[16] The original recipients of Genesis—the Israelites in the wilderness—would have heard those words and recognized something significant. The garden was God's temple. So, when an intruder comes on the scene, the original hearers know what Adam and Eve must do: drive out that serpent, keeping God's temple pure and sacred. Instead, Eve enters into a conversation with the snake, allowing the Father of Lies to lead her astray. Gladd writes, "The fall reveals that the couple failed to live up to their identity as 'images.' God designed them to rule, to worship, and to embody God's law, yet they failed . . . in all three respects."[17]

FAILURE AS PROPHETS, PRIESTS, AND KINGS

We want to make this moment of failure about Adam and Eve as man and woman, husband and wife. But Eve didn't fail as a wife; she failed as a prophet, priest, and king.[18] She isn't tempted to usurp her husband's authority; she's tempted to be like God

(Gen. 3:5). And in caving to that temptation, she brings her husband down with her. Similarly, Adam listened to Eve (Gen. 3:17) instead of driving out the serpent and clinging to and defending God's word. And he brings the whole human race down with him. Favale makes a beautiful observation here: "The woman's temptation indicates not her weakness, but rather her influence: woman's assent has the power to shape and reshape humankind."[19]

EVE'S DECEPTION AND ADAM'S RESPONSIBILITY

So, Paul points to the created order. Then he observes that Eve was deceived and became a transgressor. Why this added detail? Because it corroborates the first one. "Who cares about the created order?" some might ask (and still ask today). The first two chapters of Genesis show the man and woman to be equals, we observe. Both reflect God's image, and both are entrusted with God's mission. Paul's argument about the created order might not be sufficient to persuade us that Adam was created to be the head of the first covenant community, much less that it means there are gender-based restrictions in the church today. So, Paul turns to what happened next. Sin entered the world through Adam, not Eve, even though she was the transgressor (Rom. 5:12; 1 Tim. 2:14). *Remember guys?* he's saying. *Eve was deceived, but Adam was held responsible.*

Paul's point is not to highlight some deficiency in the female sex that prevents her from being able to teach men. Rather, he's pointing to Adam's federal headship as a paradigm for male headship in the church. Pastors do not represent us before God—Christ is the final federal head, the second Adam, our only adequate representative. But God has called qualified men to bear responsibility for those in their care. They serve as undershepherds of Christ's people and, like Adam, they will be called to give an account (1 Tim. 3:1–7; Heb. 13:17).

We'll talk more about male headship in the church and in the family, and how our role as prophets, priests, and kings looks today. But since this passage in 1 Timothy is often used to justify the story that women are the problem, we need to see what Paul is actually saying. The story that defines us is one in which God's good creation rebels against Him, but in His kindness and mercy, He works through the mess to accomplish our salvation and provide and care for us within His church.

The Curse of Sin

Our competing stories—women are the problem/men are the problem—aren't satisfied by Paul's explanation, of course. If Eve's inherent deficiencies aren't revealed in her temptation and fall, as those who see women as the problem suggest, then perhaps the female nature is corrupted because of God's curse. Human nature is certainly corrupted by sin, but some people have used the fall and curse narratives, alongside Paul's teaching in 1 Timothy 2:12–14 and elsewhere, to specify gendered propensities toward sin. Maybe the headship Paul describes is an antidote to some sort of newly wayward feminine spirit, they suggest; after all, it was she who became a transgressor (1 Tim. 2:14). Protestant Reformer John Calvin suggests that Eve willingly yielded to her husband's leadership prior to the fall, but after sin entered the world, "she is cast into servitude."[20] Modern interpretations of Eve's curse suggest that women have an inherent desire to usurp authority that doesn't belong to them.[21]

This isn't far from those who point to men as the problem: Beth Allison Barr labels Genesis 3:16 as "the biblical explanation for the birth of patriarchy."[22]

But here again we are missing the beautiful story.

HIDING IN THE BUSHES

Imagine you're Eve and you hear God coming. Do His words ring in your ears? "But of the tree of the knowledge of good and evil you shall not eat, for in the day that you eat of it you shall surely die" (Gen. 2:17). The *day* you eat of it, He said. And the day has come. So you crouch in the bushes, fear pulsating as you anticipate that your Creator, your Covenant Lord, is coming in judgment. When His voice breaks through, your breath catches as you reveal yourself in homemade clothes. Maybe you look to your husband, hoping to find solace in the man who was singing over you just a few moments ago. But instead, he speaks up, spewing blame at you. So, you bring your own excuses. *The serpent! He was so convincing! He made me doubt you!* Maybe your head hangs in shame after that. You know you're guilty. Maybe silent tears roll down your cheeks as you wait for the hammer to fall.

> **FROM ADAM AND EVE'S LINE, GOD PRESERVES A PEOPLE FOR HIMSELF FROM WHOM THE SAVIOR OF THE WORLD WOULD COME.**

THE REAL PROBLEM

The hammer does fall, but it's not where you expect. When God confronts Adam and Eve in the garden, it's not Eve who is cursed but the serpent (Gen. 3:14). And embedded in the serpent's curse is God's mercy: He will put enmity between the serpent and the woman, between his seed and hers (Gen. 3:15). This means, first of all, that a war has begun. From here, two seeds will diverge, waging battle until the very end (Rev. 12). Remember, these chapters are not primarily the foundation of our maleness or femaleness; they are the foundation of the rest of Scripture. The Old Testament unfolds to showcase this battle between two seeds—the seed of the serpent seeking to destroy the seed of the woman. But in keeping with God's promise, a faithful remnant always remains. From Adam and Eve's line, God preserves a people for Himself from whom the Savior of the world would come.

The serpent's curse also clarifies for us who the enemy is. God doesn't affirm Adam's conclusion that the woman is the problem. Instead, He shows that the serpent is. "Cursed are *you*," God speaks to the serpent (Gen. 3:14). He does pronounce judgments that affect Adam and Eve and their posterity—"I will surely multiply your pain" and "Cursed is the ground because of you" (Gen. 3:16, 17)—but only the serpent is cursed directly. The Father of Lies is the enemy, and those who align themselves with him join his ranks against their Maker. But God will not let Adam and Eve be lost to their deceiver. In declaring war against the serpent, He's also drawing a line in the sand. God will not allow his lawbreakers to be lost for good. "This one is *mine*," he tells the serpent about Eve. The woman's rebel status doesn't diminish her value to the God who made her. She may have been deceived, but He will not forfeit her to the deceiver's domain. She is worth saving.

The serpent's curse also highlights a clear difference between God's treatment of the true enemy, the serpent, and Adam and Eve. When God turns to Adam and Eve in judgment, He gives them a further glimpse into what their sin will cost. The commission He gave them—to be fruitful and multiply, to subdue the earth, to work and keep the garden—was intended to contribute to Adam and Eve's flourishing. They would thrive as they lived out their created design, spreading God's glory to the ends of the earth. But now, their mission is disrupted. Engaged in battle with the serpent, and now having to fight against their own indwelling sin and life in a fallen creation, the work that was meant to lead to their flourishing will be frustrating. And it will no longer lead to eternal gains, as we'll discuss in the next chapter. And yet, even God's judgments are couched in His mercy.

Adam and Eve's proper punishment would have been immediate death, both physical and spiritual. This was God's warning when he gave the prohibition, remember? "In the *day* that you eat of it you shall surely die" (Gen. 2:17, emphasis mine). Some argue that God had spiritual death in mind, or even eventual death. But, as Old Testament professor Joshua Van Ee writes, "It is best to say that God does not bring about the threatened judgment on the man and the woman. . . . The narrative is an example of God refraining from bringing the promised judgment as seen elsewhere in the Hebrew Bible."[23] Instead of immediate physical death, God tells the couple that life will go on. There will be pain in childbearing, but there will also be children! Though there's a lot of debate about what Genesis 3:16 means when it says, "Your desire shall be for your husband, and he shall rule over you," I think it's possible to see here God's merciful restoration. Even though childbearing will bring her pain, the woman will still desire the union through which that pain will come: marriage. And the man will still be called to exercise headship as God intended it, bearing responsibility for the well-being of his household.[24] (See the note for a fuller explanation.)

AND WHAT HAPPENED

The curse narrative doesn't present women as the problem, nor does it present men as the problem. Rather, it shows us the far-reaching effects of sin—in our hearts, relationships, bodies, and work, and with the creation that surrounds us. Adam and Eve's relationship will be marked by struggle, as will every human relationship since the garden. We've already seen a glimpse of what it looks like: shame, blame, hiding. But God doesn't inflict these punishments on Adam and Eve in the curse—they experienced them immediately upon sinning. Apart from His intervening grace, they—and we—are "dead in [our] trespasses and sins," "having no hope and without God in the world," "hated by others and hating one another" (Eph. 2:1, 12; Titus 3:3).

But, despite the continued rebellion of the human race, communal life will continue. Marriages will persist, and through this union of man and woman, God will continue to create and sustain life until the appointed time, so He can accomplish His plan of redemption. As Eve and her descendants travail in the pains of labor, they will remember what their sin cost. They will experience devastation along the way, losing children and dealing with disability, sickness, and rebellion. But each new birth will serve as a reminder of God's abundant mercy, sustaining life when it shouldn't be possible.

And these babies will have to eat. So, though the ground is now cursed as the result of sin, with thorns and thistles making the work hard and frustrating, the man and woman will eat its fruit nonetheless. "In pain *you shall eat of it all the days of your life,*" God says. "*You shall eat bread*" (Gen. 3:17, 19). We're so practiced in reading these words that we miss their significance. Here again we see God's mercy. Every day the man labors, he will feel the weight of his sin, but every bite of salad and every piece of bread will remind him that God provides for him.

THE BEAUTIFUL STORY

God does pronounce that the punishment they've escaped temporarily will now come for them: death. But even within this blow He embeds a hidden promise that will find its fullness later on in the pages of Scripture: Resurrection is coming. "For as by a man came death, by a man has come also the resurrection of the dead. For as in Adam all die, so also in Christ shall all be made alive," writes the apostle Paul (1 Cor. 15:21–22). "So is it with the resurrection of the dead. What is sown is perishable; what is raised is imperishable. It is sown in dishonor; it is raised in glory. It is sown in weakness; it is raised in power" (1 Cor. 15:42–43).

Genesis 3 shows us the devastating effects of sin, but it also shows us the restorative power of God's mercy. In a world tainted by sin, believer and unbeliever alike need God's grace to be kept from utter destruction. God's promises in Genesis 3 ground the covenant of common grace He will formalize after the flood. He will sustain humanity despite how royally they've messed everything up, because human history will be the stage upon which God brings about His promised redemption. Life must go on—with no thanks to us—until one day, through the bloody pain of childbearing, the seed of the woman will be born. That Seed will sweat and toil under the sun, accomplishing the tasks Adam couldn't. And one day, His sinful creation will press a crown of thorns into His flesh and nail Him to a cross. He will face death so that we can know resurrection.

> **HUMAN HISTORY WILL BE THE STAGE UPON WHICH GOD BRINGS ABOUT HIS PROMISED REDEMPTION.**

The beautiful story of the gospel is right there, from the beginning. God's mercy re-stories us, beckoning us to reject the narratives that leave us pointing fingers from the bushes.

Adam responds to the curse narrative with faith. Meredith Kline writes, "Adam in effect declared his confessional 'Amen' to the Genesis 3:15 promise of restoration from death to life through the woman's seed. This he did by naming the woman

'Life' (Eve)."[25] I would argue that Adam is responding to the whole confrontation—the delay of death, the hope of continued life and provision, and God's promise of a deliverer. Eve is a fitting name for His bride as he receives her back, restored to him to live together as sinners in view of God's mercies. Life after the fall is an act of God's grace, to which Adam responds, "Amen!" And so should we.

Sin's Sprawling Story

I sometimes wonder if we're tempted to accept a competing narrative because it feels more aligned with our lived experiences, more honest about just how devastating and far-reaching sin's effects are. We want to understand why there are women who usurp authority, who leverage their sex appeal to ensnare, who shy away from theology, or who spend their days engaged in gossip and worldly pursuits. We want an explanation for abusive men who pursue and exploit power, for misogyny and sexism, and for the ways women are oppressed and mistreated, exploited and silenced.

Proclaiming the story of God's abundant mercy doesn't deny these things exist, but it reorients how we think about them. Genesis 3 is the origin story for the sin we see in ourselves and in those around us, but its goal is not to create neat definitions for gendered propensities toward sin. If we want to fill out the picture of sin's effects, we need to keep reading beyond Genesis 3.

TWO SEEDS

After the fall, we see the first whisper of God's promise come to fruition: "Now Adam knew Eve his wife, and she conceived and bore Cain, saying, 'I have gotten a man with the help of the LORD.' And again, she bore his brother Abel" (Gen. 4:1–2). We learn quickly that Cain and Abel (later replaced by Seth) will be

STORIED

the head of two lines—the two seeds introduced to us in God's promise of Genesis 3:15. And those seeds are going to battle.

God is pleased with Abel and his offering, but not with Cain's (Gen. 4:4–5). Like his parents in the garden, Cain refuses to heed God's word. He kills Abel and tries to bury the evidence (Gen. 4:8–11). He, too, is confronted by God. But here, God shows that Cain has aligned himself with the serpent when He pronounces direct judgment on Cain (Gen. 4:11).[26]

Despite Cain's treacherous alliance, God in His common grace preserves Cain's line. He sends him away, but He allows the seed of the serpent to grow. His descendants build cities and make music. But it's also worth noting that Lamech descends from Cain, and his boastful pronouncement recorded in Genesis 4:23–24 contains the Bible's first mention of polygamy and injustice. Sin reigns among the serpent's seed, and this is set up in contrast to Seth and his line, from whom "people began to call upon the name of the LORD" (Gen. 4:26). As Genesis unfolds, rather than showing us a battle of the sexes, the narrative often uses the conflict between brothers to draw out the tension of God's warring seeds.

The point of showing these contrasting lines in Genesis 4 and elsewhere isn't to say that the faithful seed will be immune from sin and its consequences. It's not that one seed is all good and the other is all bad. When we get to Genesis 6, sin has become so rampant that the earth is filled with violence and corruption (Gen. 6:11–12). It seems like the serpent's seed has pulled ahead, and God's faithful line is in danger of being completely wiped out. But God has made a promise, and He preserves Noah through the flood. It quickly becomes clear, however, that this fresh start didn't solve the problem of sin. The narrative exposes Noah's flaws (Gen. 9:21–22) while also showing that Noah's grandson Canaan will carry on the serpent's seed. Like the serpent and Cain, Canaan receives a direct curse (Gen. 9:25) and his genealogy positions him at the head of the nations who will become enemies of God's people (Gen. 10:15–20).

THE PROMISED SEED

As the story continues, God's promises become more specific. He chooses a family through whom His deliverer will come, making a covenant with Abraham, Isaac, and Jacob. Over and over, the effects of sin in the world threaten to undermine God's plan of salvation. We sit on the edge of our seats, wondering if the promised Seed is going to make it to the last pages of Genesis, much less through the rest of the Bible. Along the way, we see the high points of the curse reverberate—infertility, land disputes, and famine are now commonplace in a fallen world. Conflict, violence, and corruption are new markers of this sinful reality. And the text does tell some dark stories, both about the mistreatment of women—such as how Abraham and Isaac both pretend their wives are their sisters, Hagar's sad story, Jacob's polygamous marriage, cruelty toward Leah, the sexual assault of Dinah, and the exploitation of Tamar—and women's mistreatment of others—like Sarah with Hagar, Rebekah deceiving Isaac, Rachel and Leah's rivalry, and Potiphar's wife. But Genesis doesn't seem to be highlighting gendered propensities, pointing to either men or women as the problem. Instead, it's showing the grim human tendency toward sin. Sin is the enemy, its veiny tentacles wrapped around every human heart. Yet God is faithful. He keeps His promise, tenaciously preserving His seed despite their—men *and* women's—every effort to make His plans fail.

Sinful Manhood and Womanhood

If sin is the problem, then we're not somehow absolved, as if it's this abstract force outside of us. No, if sin is the problem, then men *and* women are the problem too.

As we look to the biblical narrative for truth about what God is saying about His fallen image bearers, we shouldn't take from this story that we're innocent bystanders. My point has never been to argue that either women or men are somehow more virtuous than others say. If anything, my goal has been to show that we can sin in much greater ways than we'd care to admit. We walk in the footsteps of our forebears. Abusive men and usurping women are real. (So are abusive women and usurping men.) In many more ways, we are guilty, caught with blood on our hands. Sin taints our actions, motives, and assumptions about one another. We're left with no cause for pointing fingers. If I want to get to the bottom of what's wrong with the world, I need to start with myself.

Nonetheless, the story of God's people is a redemptive one. Genesis 1–3 shows creation's formation, undoing, and restoration. Sin will play an ugly, domineering role, but it will not have the final say. If we come to this story to figure out what it's saying about being a man or a woman without taking in this big picture, we'll miss the punch line: "We are more sinful and flawed in ourselves than we ever dared believe," Tim Keller writes, "yet at the very same time we are more loved and accepted in Jesus Christ than we ever dared hope.[27]

Daughters of Eve, Restored

Sister Grace Remington, a Cistercian nun at Our Lady of the Mississippi Abbey in Iowa, has a drawing she affectionately calls "The Ladies." In it, a pregnant Mary consoles Eve, her foot crushing the serpent's head. The snake winds around Eve's leg as she clutches the forbidden fruit and reaches out to Mary's bulging belly, the secret home of the Savior of the world. Eve's face is filled with grief, while Mary's holds compassion for her fallen forebear.

"One of the things I was pondering as I drew this picture was the question of why Eve said 'no' to God and Mary said 'yes,'" Sister Grace says. "I started to think about how Eve had no idea what it would mean to live in a fallen world, to be separated from God."[28] She continues,

> *I wondered whether Mary was able to give her yes precisely because she knew the pain of life. She knew how desperately we needed God. Her eyes were open. This was part of what I see as her compassion for Eve in this picture. She is not standing with folded hands on a pedestal above Eve: she is standing with Eve, touching Eve, seeing her deeply. She knows the gift she is carrying is for Eve as much as it is for herself. She doesn't need Eve to get herself together, or to even drop the apple before inviting her in.*[29]

I can't look at Sister Grace's drawing without being moved to tears. For all my love for Dottie Hinson and Sydney Bristow, I feel more affinity with my mother Eve. I resonate with her shame, but I admire her perseverance. I learn from her about God's mercy, about what courage and faith look like in a fallen world. Though I'm intimately acquainted with doubt in God's goodness and my propensity for wandering, and though I feel the serpent's grip and grieve my sin and its effects around me, I choose to believe the better story, looking with hope to that Promised Seed.

4

Commissioned

ON DOING WORK THAT MATTERS

It is in vain to say human beings ought to be satisfied with tranquility: they must have action; and they will make it if they cannot find it.

JANE EYRE

Up to this point, I've sought to address some of our existential crises, to help us focus on our inherent dignity, our essential presence. We've had to reexamine our biblical interpretation, seeing how our understanding of the story unfolding in the first few chapters of Genesis colors the lens through which we'll view the rest of Scripture, as well as our life experiences.

But if you're anything like me, you're starting to get restless. It brings relief to shine a light on the narratives that have left us cowering in the shadows. We rejoice at what's true, that God created us in His image and has redeemed us by the blood of His Son. Yet we still want to know what happens when our feet hit the pavement. "How we spend our days is, of course, how we spend our lives," writes Annie Dillard, and we feel this acutely.[1] We're deeply concerned with how we ought to spend our days.

We can't stop at value; we need to talk about vocation.

Holistic Image-Bearing

We've seen that image-bearing is holistic—it's about who we are, but also about what we do. Unfortunately, whenever we talk about a woman's vocation, we get a little twisted. We become more concerned with boxing one another in or keeping each other out. We see vocation like a pie with only so many slices, and we can't help but wonder, *Why does yours look bigger than mine?* The thread between our *being* and *doing* gets pulled so tight we're afraid it might snap. We wonder what it says about us if we can or can't do something. What value is tied to the nature of our work? (And, let's be honest, it doesn't help anything that "women's work" isn't usually a term reserved for tasks held in high esteem.)

God's commission to Adam and Eve in Genesis grounds many an explanation for our continued purpose as humans and the specific roles we play as men and women. Perhaps we view Adam's and Eve's functions as abiding, labeling all men as leaders and all women as helpers. Or maybe we assume their commissioned work is gender-specific, concluding the man's primary function is to "subdue" (in other words, *work*), and the woman's primary work is to "fill" (in other words, *have babies*). But here again our interpretations are often reductionistic, trying to make the Bible answer the questions of our day.[2]

We need to revisit Genesis 1–3 again, applying another principle of biblical interpretation we've been subtly employing thus far: We must understand Scripture in its context.[3] We need to think about what the author intended and how the original audience would have heard and applied it. In other words, as we look again at the early chapters of the Bible, we need to understand the original intent of Adam and Eve's mandate and consider the impact of its post-fall distortion. *Then* we get to us.

To help us do that, we need to weave together the covenantal threads we've located in Genesis 1–3. Recall some of the things we've highlighted so far: These chapters aren't written merely to show us what it means to be a man or woman, but to make theological points, setting the stage for redemptive history. Image-bearing, Adam's headship, the first couple's commission, their fall into sin, and even God's pronouncement of judgment are all presented in the context of covenant.

Basically, we've been dipping our toes into what is known as covenant theology, a framework for understanding Scripture that recognizes covenants as the Bible's foundational structure. God relates to His people through covenants, and it's through this progression of covenants that redemptive history unfolds. Now I want to dive in, to bring these themes together in order to look more closely at their implications for our modern-day mission. We'll look at how covenant theology helps reframe our under-standing of headship and helping, fruitfulness and work, and we'll find that, as a result, it also reframes our womanhood, pre-paring us to fulfill our callings with courage.

The Covenant of Works

We were created to work. We feel it in our souls—we want to be useful, to contribute something meaningful. This is God's design for how we live out our image-bearing nature. The creation narrative presents God as a worker, steadily laboring, surveying His efforts, and then resting. He creates Adam and Eve to follow this pattern: He created them to *be* like Him, but He also created them to *do* like Him, as we've seen, to image Him as prophets, priests, and kings.

That job wasn't just for fun. Adam and Eve's pre-fall commission had an end in mind. Yes, they needed "to make creation a livable place for humans," but this was so "they would achieve the grand aim of glorifying [God]."[4] When they succeeded, they would enter God's rest. They would achieve eternal glory—a perfected state that was better than Eden. This is what theologians call the "covenant of works," the implicit covenant God makes with Adam at creation.[5] In their primer on covenant theology, *Sacred Bond*, Michael Brown and Zach Keele describe the covenant of works like this:

> *At creation, God commits himself to his creation to sustain them and be God to them. So also, being created in the image of God by necessity obligates Adam to God. In Genesis 1:26, God fashions male and female in his image so that they may have dominion, which is an obligation. God's act of creation generates a relationship with implicit obligations, namely, to imitate God.*[6]

We saw in chapter 2 that, as the first one created, Adam was our *federal head*—our representative in the covenant of works. If Adam had perfectly and perpetually obeyed God's commands, he would have successfully lived out his commission alongside his God-given partner, resulting in eternal life for the first couple and their posterity.[7] But we also saw what happened instead—as head of the human race, when Adam failed, we all fell with him. Brown and Keele explain, "Quite simply, this means the consequences of Adam's actions were . . . passed on to his children. If he earned life, he earned it for himself and all his descendants, and so also with death. This aspect of the covenant is obvious from human history. Once Adam fell, death came to Eve, Cain, and Abel, even to all mankind (Rom. 5:12)."[8]

We tend to overlook the context of Genesis and see in Adam's role as head and Eve's as helper an enduring principle about maleness and femaleness. Instead, one of the first applications to draw from this covenantal backdrop is the way it reframes headship and helping as covenantal functions.

Reframing Headship

Let's first consider that headship is a function of God's covenant with Adam. It defines God's way of dealing with His people corporately. This makes us a little uncomfortable as those who like to think of ourselves as free and independent, but we've already seen that this is good news. We need a representative! Speaking of Paul's explanation of the two Adams in Romans, New Testament scholar Douglas Moo writes, "The perspective is corporate rather than individual." He continues,

> *All people, Paul teaches, stand in relationship to one of two men, whose actions determine the eternal destiny of all who belong to them. Either one "belongs to" Adam and is under sentence of death because of his sin, or disobedience, or one belongs to Christ and is assured of eternal life because of his "righteous" act, or obedience.*[9]

If we don't grasp our relationship to the first and second Adams, we miss the incredible work God did when He sent Christ to rescue us. We need to understand the crucial theological concept of imputation, which says Adam's sin is credited to us because he was representing all humankind when he disobeyed God in the garden. And in the same way, by faith, Christ's righteousness also is credited to us. This is the doctrine of justification.

That means we all—male and female—exist under headship. Christ is our head. We died in Adam, but in Christ, we're made alive (1 Cor. 15:21–22). Headship is first and foremost a function of God's covenant.

REPRESENTATION AND RESPONSIBILITY

As headship persists after the garden, there are some shifts in how we apply it. *Federal headship* served a purpose of both representation and responsibility. Adam represented all humanity before God, and he bore responsibility for his—and Eve's—failure. The Old Testament continues to provide a covenant head through whom God relates to His people, like Abraham, Isaac, Jacob, Moses, and David, "that by the one the many received the promised inheritance," as S. M. Baugh writes.[10]

These covenant heads proved unable to fulfill Adam's commission, but they pointed forward to Christ, who came and completed Adam's work once and for all, initiating a new covenant by His blood.

Now that Christ has come, we all continue to relate to God through a representative, but as Moo noted above, there are only two options: Adam or Christ. So the purpose of headship today is not to represent us as a mediator before God; Christ is the final federal head. *He's* our representative, bearing the punishment we deserve, and presenting His own righteousness on our behalf: "For there is one God, and there is one mediator between God and men, the man Christ Jesus, who gave himself as a ransom for all" (1 Tim. 2:5–6a). We are born in Adam, but by faith, we are united to Christ and indwelled by His Spirit, receiving His work on our behalf.

When we view headship in its covenantal context, it gives us a fuller picture of its purpose in Genesis and aids our application as we go from there. With the representative function fulfilled in Christ, the enduring function of headship is about corporate responsibility.

BENEVOLENT LEADERSHIP

Despite the ongoing destruction of sin, authority post-Eden is appointed by God and intended to bring order to society, providing for the good of those under its protective care. Think of this as ordinary, not federal, headship. God Himself provides the pattern for this kind of patient, wise, and benevolent leadership. He is the compassionate Father, "merciful and gracious, slow to anger and abounding in steadfast love" (Ps. 103:8, 13). He is the faithful husband, the just judge, the protector, provider, sustainer, and refuge of His people.

We're prone to think about authority in terms of power and privilege, focusing on its sinful distortion in the form of selfishness, oppression, exploitation, and abuse. But historian Daniel Block warns against this misunderstanding of the Bible's teaching about headship. He writes, "We do a disservice to the biblical record if we are preoccupied with the power the [husband or father] wielded. In healthy and functional households the male head was neither despot nor dictator. On the contrary, since the family members were perceived as extensions of the progenitor's own life, the head's own interests depended upon the well-being of the household."[11] Block continues,

> *Rather than evoking images of "ruler" or "boss," the [Hebrew word for father] expressed confidence, trust and security. This emphasis on the responsibilities associated with headship over the household (as opposed to its privileges and power) is consistent with the overall tenor of the Old Testament, which views leadership in general to be a privilege granted to an individual in order to serve the interests of those who are led.*

Christ's life, ministry, and work of redemption ultimately completes the picture of how headship is meant to be

A PLACE FOR YOU

practiced—through self-sacrificing love (Eph. 5:25–30), just as
He taught His disciples:

> *"You know that the rulers of the Gentiles lord it over them,
> and their great ones exercise authority over them. It shall not
> be so among you. But whoever would be great among you
> must be your servant, and whoever would be first among you
> must be your slave, even as the Son of Man came not to be
> served but to serve, and to give his life as a ransom for many."*
> (Matt. 20:25–28)

In the ordinary headship that persists after the garden, the enduring principle isn't primarily about gender but function. Though
ancient Near Eastern and Greco-Roman societies were patriarchal, the Bible still offers examples of women who served as civil
leaders (Judg. 5:14–15; Mic. 6:4), household managers (Gen.
16:6; Prov. 31:15), and businesswomen (Prov. 31:16–19; Acts
16:14–15; 18:1–3). Anyone who serves in a leadership capacity,
male or female, should take to heart the principles for leadership
found in *federal headship*, where the Bible emphasizes responsibility, accountability, sacrifice, and seeking the well-being of those
under your care.

INSTITUTIONS, NOT GENDER

It's important that we connect these dots between the purpose
of Genesis, Adam's federal headship, the functions of representation and responsibility, and the broad application of leadership
throughout Scripture. If we don't, we'll find ourselves swimming
in the poor interpretations we saw in chapter 3. We'll start to
believe that Adam's headship is based on his maleness, that this
implies some inherent characteristic within all males that gives

COMMISSIONED

them authority over all females. We'll view leadership or authority held by a woman as suspect, or we'll question whether godly authority is even a feasible reality, relegating any exercise of such as patriarchy or abuse.

The New Testament does prescribe two areas where headship is restricted to certain male candidates, in the church and home. But it's noteworthy that these areas of headship are tied to institutions, not gender. Male headship within households relates to the function of being a husband. I know it sounds like I'm mincing words—obviously husbands are male!—but by rooting the authority in the function, we see the point that not all males are heads of all females; all *husbands* are heads of *their own families* (1 Cor. 11:3; Eph. 5:23). Similarly, headship in the church is reserved for *qualified* men who are appointed to the office of elder (1 Tim. 2:12–3:7); it's not passed out to all men broadly.[12] Not all men will exercise headship, and those who do are not handed unchecked power but an immense responsibility to care for those entrusted to them, as the apostle Peter instructs: "Shepherd the flock of God that is among you, exercising oversight, not under compulsion, but willingly, as God would have you; not for shameful gain, but eagerly; not domineering over those in your charge, but being examples to the flock" (1 Peter 5:2–3).

A LOOK AT THE RECORD

Some question if we should see the New Testament's teaching about male headship in the church and home as still being applicable today, claiming that any system of gender-based headship is oppressive to women. And, as we've noted, sin's effects are certainly far-reaching, with plenty of examples of distorted and harmful applications. Nonetheless, throughout history, the church has provided a refuge from society's misogyny. "Christianity is predominantly female," Jen Oshman writes, drawing on the work of sociologist and historian Rodney Stark to highlight the church's record of elevating women in contrast to their secular counterparts.[13] In fact, we could argue that women's rights are an inherently Christian idea.[14] Wherever Christianity spread, the dignity and rights of women grew.

This is seen not only in the historical record, but in the biblical texts themselves. In ancient Rome, household codes addressed the head of the household—the man. He held the power of life and death over his household. Women and children were considered less than human, having no rights of their own. So when the apostles Peter and Paul write their household codes in Ephesians, Colossians, and 1 Peter, addressing not only husbands and fathers, but also wives and mothers and children, they are making a bold statement, asserting the personhood and agency of each member of the household, ensuring their safety, and providing boundaries around the exercise of headship.

The same can be said regarding New Testament texts that restrict women's participation as officers in the church. We'll look at these passages in more detail in chapter 8, but it's noteworthy that the Bible welcomes women in gathered worship, encourages their learning and discipleship, and celebrates their participation in the ministry of the church. In these contexts, male headship, when practiced rightly, does not oppress women, it elevates them.

The point of all this is twofold: We need to recognize that, one, the presentation of Adam's headship in Genesis is not establishing a normative function for all men in all contexts. Rather, it's setting the foundation for redemptive history by presenting Adam as federal head and laying the covenantal foundation of one for the many, leading us to Christ.

And two, the biblical principles guiding headship are representation and responsibility, not power and privilege.

COMMISSIONED

Reframing Helping

Helping can be viewed in this same covenantal context. In Moses' zoomed-out scene of Genesis 1, we see that Adam and Eve both receive God's commission: "Be fruitful and multiply and fill the earth and subdue it, and have dominion over the fish of the sea and over the birds of the heavens and over every living thing that moves on the earth" (Gen. 1:28). This set of instructions is known as the cultural mandate.

In the zoomed-in story of Genesis 2, Adam receives more detailed instructions that highlight his role as a priest to guard God's temple and identify the testing ground for his covenant faithfulness, the tree of the knowledge of good and evil (Gen. 2:15–17).

"HELPER" IS NOT ABOUT WOMANHOOD

The second set of instructions further fills out God's instructions for His image bearers, and it immediately precedes God's declaration, "It is not good that the man should be alone; I will make him a helper fit for him" (Gen. 2:18). This anchors Eve's role as a helper in God's covenant with Adam. Elizabeth Garn writes,

> *Adam didn't need a pretty face or even a friend to fill some emotional void. It wasn't his loneliness or his need for a companion that necessitated the woman, it was his calling. He wasn't just alone in the garden; he was alone in his mission.*[15]

We've seen that this word "helper" does not describe a diminished role. To be a helper is to be a covenantal partner. God made Eve to come alongside Adam and help him succeed in the tasks God had given them, for which Adam would be held

81

accountable. We said in the previous chapter that Eve didn't fail as a wife—she failed as a prophet, priest, and king. But it would also be right to say that in failing as a prophet, priest, and king, she failed as a covenantal helper. Her job was to help Adam keep his eye on the prize, to achieve eternal life for both of them. But instead, she handed him the forbidden fruit.

EVE WAS TO PARTNER WITH ADAM SO THEY COULD FULFILL THE CULTURAL MANDATE.

This covenantal context once again reframes how we think about function and application. Here, we see that covenantal helping isn't rooted in female nature but in the corporate mission.

This should be an easier conclusion to reach because we've already seen how the most commonly named Helper in Scripture is God Himself. Yet that hasn't stopped people from concluding that Eve as helper means helping is a strictly feminine calling.

However, Eve's help had a specific end in mind. She was to partner with Adam so they could fulfill the cultural mandate, pass the test, and achieve eternal life for themselves and their posterity. Her helping was essential because spreading God's glory to the ends of the earth was a momentous task that required more than one person. Eve's very body was essential—Adam quite literally could not "be fruitful and multiply" without her—but, often overlooked, Adam also needed her partnership. Eve offered complementary perspective, strengths, and skills to carry out God's mission.

HELPING AS THE FRAMEWORK FOR COMMUNITY

After the fall, helping isn't restricted to women for men. Instead, it's the framework given for community life. One example comes in

Exodus, when "Moses sat to judge the people, and the people stood around Moses from morning till evening" (Ex. 18:13). Watching this take place, Moses' father-in-law asks a question that echoes God's words in Genesis 2:18, that it is "not good" for the man to be "alone."[16] "Why do you sit alone? . . . What you are doing is not good. You and the people with you will certainly wear yourselves out, for the thing is too heavy for you. You are not able to do it alone" (Ex. 18:14, 17–18). He recognizes that the task is too great for Moses to bear alone, so he advises him to get help:

> "Look for able men from all the people, men who fear God, who are trustworthy and hate a bribe, and place such men over the people as chiefs of thousands, of hundreds, of fifties, and of tens. And let them judge the people at all times. . . . So it will be easier for you, and they will bear the burden with you." (Ex. 18:21–22)

Here's a picture of headship and helping in a broad sense, distributing the work for the benefit of the community, and in this case, both roles (head and helper) are filled by men.

Helping one another is a call placed upon all God's people. The apostle Paul writes, "In all things I have shown you that by working hard in this way we must help the weak and remember the words of the Lord Jesus, how he himself said, 'It is more blessed to give than to receive'" (Acts 20:35). All Christians are called to serve one another through love (Gal. 5:13), and "helping" is listed as a special gift given by God's Spirit (1 Cor. 12:28). The Westminster Confession of Faith even applies this language broadly to marriage, saying, "Marriage was ordained for the *mutual help* of husband and wife."[17]

GOD INVITES US INTO HIS MISSION

There is still a way that covenantal helping plays out as God's redeemed people labor side by side for the sake of the gospel. Christ our groom is at work, gathering His people from every tribe, tongue, and nation that He might "present the church to himself in splendor" (Eph. 5:27). He commissions us to help Him carry out His mission: "Go therefore and make disciples of all nations, baptizing them in the name of the Father and of the Son and of the Holy Spirit, teaching them to observe all that I have commanded you. And behold, I am with you always, to the end of the age" (Matt. 28:19–20). Empowered by the Helper Himself, the New Testament describes both men and women as being called to and engaged in this task (Rom. 16:1–16).

All this serves our ultimate aim of thinking through a woman's vocation. It's essential to grasp that the roles of "head" and "helper" are not meant to spell out the details of masculinity and femininity, but rather to teach us about how God orders His creation, relates to His people, and invites us on His mission.

Reframing Fruitfulness

So now we need to talk about the mission. Our covenantal backdrop reorients how we think about the cultural mandate. Adam and Eve's original commission in the covenant of works served both natural and spiritual purposes. They literally needed to fill the earth, and in this sense, fruitfulness ties directly to childbearing.

It's not limited to babies, though, since the command also meant they would be concerned with the fruitfulness of creation and the flourishing of society and culture. Their fruitfulness also had a spiritual dimension: As Adam and Eve's family grew, they would fill the earth with worshipers of God and expand His temple to the ends of the earth.[18] This overlap of natural and redemptive endeavors necessarily shifts after humanity's fall into sin. Where our efforts would have been both temporally and eternally fruitful, now those efforts are fractured. Two parallel streams flow from Eden, creating two planes on which we build our lives—the natural order and the eternal one. As Christians, we still participate in both, but with some important differences.[19]

NATURAL ORDER AND ETERNAL ORDER

In the natural, or common kingdom, we participate in the work of culture-building and contribute to the flourishing of human society alongside our neighbors, believers and unbelievers. The curse narrative in Genesis reframes the commission for a post-fall reality. God had told Adam and Eve, "Be fruitful and multiply and fill the earth," but after sin enters the world, there will be "pain in childbearing" (Gen. 1:28; 3:16). He'd also told them to subdue the earth, to work and keep the garden, but after sin enters the world, they will sweat and toil amid thorns and thistles (Gen. 1:28; 2:15; 3:17–19).

We saw the mercy embedded in this text, but we're also meant to notice how the curse mirrors the commission. There's a functional element to what's required, but the eternal reward held out in the covenant of works is gone. Humans will still need to fill the earth, and someone will have to feed all those

WE LIVE ALONGSIDE OUR NEIGHBORS IN THE NATURAL ORDER, BUT WE'RE SIMULTANEOUSLY CITIZENS OF A REDEMPTIVE KINGDOM.

people (and all the mothers said, "Amen"). But now the commission is about survival. After a long life of toil and trouble, people will return to the dust (Gen. 3:19).

As those who have been united to Christ, we live alongside our neighbors in the natural order, but we're simultaneously citizens of a redemptive kingdom. Constituted and commissioned to worship and glorify our King, we are to continue in fruitfulness, but the commission takes on a spiritual dimension, referring not to the birth of babies or the flourishing of earthly culture but to the growth of the church as people become members through faith.

AN ASIDE ABOUT MOTHERHOOD

It's worth leaning in here for a moment, since "fruitfulness" is often defined as having babies and held up as a woman's ultimate calling, how she "arrives" in womanhood. Even as we strive to love the single and childless in our midst, we need not downplay the beauty and importance of motherhood.

Though "fruitfulness" in this sense is something we share with the common realm, I believe there can be something redemptive about childbearing as God grows His church by adding members to believers' families. And, whether you count these tiny members among Christ's visible church from birth or wait for their faith to be expressed, it's a beautiful thing when a child can be raised in the nurture and admonition of the Lord amid a community of biological and spiritual family. Those Christian families called by God to raise children can be engaged in incredibly fruitful, spiritual work.

But we also must recognize that childbearing served a particular role in redemptive history. God's people live on this eternal plane under His covenant of grace, God's promise after the fall to provide a Savior through the very commission His people have failed to achieve. Genesis 3:15 promises that this Savior will come *through the seed of the woman,* and He will rule over the serpent, subduing him once and for all.

COMMISSIONED

THE UNIQUE ROLE OF MOTHERS IN REDEMPTIVE HISTORY

Childbearing is not one-to-one from Genesis to today, however, and here's why: The covenant of grace develops over the course of redemptive history. There's continuity from God's promise to Adam and Eve in Genesis 3:15 to Christ's incarnation (Luke 2:7) to His death on the cross, when He—the Seed of the woman—though bruised by the serpent, ultimately crushed his head (Luke 23:46; 24:5–7). Through this period of history, the faithful fruitfulness of God's people serves a particular redemptive purpose. Through the seed of the woman, the Savior of the world would come.

That means that, though all people are invited into the common task of continuing the human race, God's covenant community bore children in faith, looking for His promised Rescuer. I think this is what Paul is pointing to in the challenging verse, "Yet she will be saved through childbearing—if they continue in faith and love and holiness, with self-control" (1 Tim. 2:15). He's highlighting the unique role of mothers in redemptive history who bore children in faith, trusting in God's promises to sustain His line of promise, clinging to their inheritance among God's people, and

> **FAITHFUL WOMEN CONTINUE TO PRODUCE FRUITFUL LIVES NOT JUST THROUGH HAVING CHILDREN, BUT THROUGH FAITH AND LOVE AND HOLINESS.**

ultimately hoping for the Messiah foretold in Genesis 3:15. Through that childbearing, we are saved.[20] He's also showing how fruitfulness is reframed in light of the new covenant: Faithful women continue to produce fruitful lives not just through having children, but through bearing the fruit of the Holy Spirit, in faith and love and holiness, with self-control.

CHILDBEARING IN REDEMPTIVE HISTORY

There's another aspect of covenant theology that's worth pointing out when we consider the role of childbearing in redemptive history. Under the Mosaic covenant, if the people obeyed, they would "abound in prosperity, in the fruit of your womb and in the fruit of your livestock and in the fruit of your ground, within the land that the LORD swore to your fathers to give you" (Deut. 28:11). But if they disobeyed, "Cursed shall be the fruit of your womb and the fruit of your ground, the increase of your herds and the young of your flock" (Deut. 28:18). That meant fruitfulness was a sign of God's covenant blessings.

If you had lots of children, then, under the Mosaic covenant, it showed God's blessing upon you. And, after the Israelites subdued the promised land, having children meant a continued inheritance in the land. Consider that context as you read this oft-quoted verse about the blessing of children: "Behold, children are a heritage from the LORD, the fruit of the womb a reward" (Ps. 127:3). Under the Mosaic covenant, children were quite literally a heritage (or inheritance) from the Lord. It meant the family would stay on the land God had given to their fathers.

IN CHRIST, WE DON'T LIVE UNDER THE BLESSINGS AND CURSES OF THE MOSAIC COVENANT.

This is not to say there's not a continued sense in which children are a blessing from the Lord, as I've already said. But it *is* to say that, in Christ, we don't live under the blessings and curses of the Mosaic covenant. The Israelites failed to keep the Mosaic covenant and so brought the covenant curses upon themselves. But "Christ redeemed us from the curse of the law by becoming a curse for us" (Gal. 3:13). He perfectly fulfilled the requirements of the Mosaic covenant, thus securing for us "every spiritual blessing in the heavenly places" (Eph. 1:3).

"Be Fruitful and Multiply"

Having children (or not) no longer testifies to our faith in God's covenant or God's favor upon us. It's a calling God gives to some and not others, not a measure of our faith or our womanhood. But the Bible's command to "be fruitful and multiply" both continues and transforms from the Old Testament to the New. When it's tied to God's covenant of grace, the agent shifts.

Originally, God commanded Adam and Eve to be fruitful and multiply (Gen. 1:28), and we saw this formula repeated to Noah after the flood (Gen. 9:1, 7). In both instances, the objective is clear: The empty earth needed filling. But when God reveals more about His covenant of grace, identifying Abraham, Isaac, and Jacob as the line through which His promised Seed will arrive, fruitfulness "becomes more something God does for them than what they do for God."[21] On this plane, it's also no longer about filling the earth, as David VanDrunen writes:

> *What explains these developments? God is now advancing his plan of salvation. At creation, sinless human beings were to subdue, exercise dominion, and fill the earth, as their obligation before God.... But now, in the Abrahamic covenant, God set a redemptive hope before Abraham's line. God promised a seed, or offspring, through which the world would be blessed, and by believing this promise, Abraham was justified (Gen. 15:5–6). This picked up the original gospel promise of Genesis 3:15, in which God pledged that the seed of the woman would crush the head of the serpent. Paul, in turn, picked up this line of thought by declaring Christ the seed God promised to Abraham (Gal. 3:16).[22]*

VanDrunen highlights two main differences in the "fruitful and multiply" formula between its earlier iterations and its encounter with Abraham:

> *First, because salvation is a divine work, God says that he will make Abraham and his line fruitful. Second, the reason there's no interest here in filling the earth is because God will accomplish his plan of salvation through building Israel as a holy nation in a holy land, in which context God will bring forth the promised Messianic seed of Eve/Abraham.*

After Christ comes, there's another shift. Christ is the Promised Seed to whom all the promises pointed, and His life and death inaugurate a new era of His covenant of grace. The Bible never again tells God's people to "be fruitful and multiply," but this language does show up in the New Testament. It's still what God does in and through His people.

GOD'S WORD: FRUITFUL AND MULTIPLYING

G. K. Beale observes that the book of Acts references Genesis 1:28, but it's God's Word that's fruitful and multiplying (see Acts 6:7; 12:24; and 19:20).[23] The apostle Paul writes about the gospel "bearing fruit and increasing," causing the church to "[bear] fruit in every good work and [increase] in the knowledge of God" (Col. 1:6, 10).[24] Through the proclamation of this word and the faithful witness of this church, God will add to its numbers. As Christians, we get to be a part of this fruitful work of Christ by His Spirit both as recipients and agents. We are given a "new self, which is being renewed in knowledge after the image of its creator" (Col. 3:10), and so we continue bearing God's image as prophets, priests, and kings in His spiritual kingdom, confessing

His name, offering our bodies as living sacrifices to God, and fighting against the world, the flesh, and the devil in this life, until we reign with Christ forever.[25]

When we view the cultural mandate covenantally, it confronts our temptation to view motherhood as a woman's only option for faithful contribution. Fruitfulness is still part of bearing God's image on both the natural plane and the eternal one, but we need to account for shifts over the course of redemptive history. Where the Old Testament had no category for singleness, the New Testament commends the single-minded devotion to Christ afforded singles (1 Cor. 7:8), just as it commends marriage and family life for those who desire it (1 Cor. 7:9; 1 Tim. 5:14). Both are seen as appointed by God, and in His hands, can bear much fruit.

In pragmatic terms, society continues to function well with healthy families at its core. The population needs to be regularly replaced for life to continue. Children are a gift from the Lord, and motherhood is a viable vocation that's only available to women. It is good and true to say and celebrate those things, even perhaps to challenge some of the ways we might have adopted the world's thinking and spurned the good gifts of marriage and childbearing. And yet, for all intents and purposes, the earth is full, but Christ is not done building His church. He calls us to join Him in His work of making disciples, promising that as some plant and others water, God will give the growth (1 Cor. 3:6–7).

Reframing Work

This excursion through covenant theology offers another shift in perspective before we get practical. The covenants also reframe how we think about work. Even though Adam and Eve failed to fulfill the covenant of works, unable to achieve eternal life by their works, that didn't render it obsolete. Instead, we're all born into it. We still bear God's image, and we feel the weight of its inherent obligations.

The longing for meaningful, productive, and eternal work is written on our hearts. But now we're also born into Adam's sin. So, though we work—and work *hard*—we do so knowing deep down we don't measure up. That's the source of our hustling and clawing and pulsating despair. It's why we're working so hard to carve out our place, to make sure it's big enough. We're trying to prove we deserve to be here. We're trying to build something that lasts. Left to our own devices, we'll become like Sisyphus, pushing our rock up the hill as if it's not just going to roll down again.

THE "FUTILITY" OF WORK?

The Preacher in Ecclesiastes is a master at showing us our feeble attempts at meaning through the works of our hands. We were created to do work that reaps eternal rewards, and that's why the Preacher is so frustrated when he encounters the futility of his labors. *Nothing lasts!* he laments, and we join him. We know the toil and pain of work under the sun, all our efforts wasted. Your best ideas executed by someone who will claim the credit. Your blood, sweat, and tears invested in a company that will be sold to the highest bidder, your loyalty met with a layoff. Your daily labors in feeding and clothing all those people, only to stare at more dishes in the sink, laundry on the floor, and hungry kids looking for lunch.

We need to address our tendency to make our work say something about us, because if we don't, we'll keep arguing past each other. If we haven't embraced the value of our being, we'll look to our work to prove we're valuable to others. If we're still living under a covenant of works, we'll also look to our work to prove we're valuable to God. In either case, we'll view any restrictions as an assault on our dignity and worth, and we'll miss the point of our work in this world.

To get there, we need to see that Christ accomplished the work we couldn't. Only His work can last forever. Only His work has anything to say about who we are and what we're worth. Christ fulfilled the covenant of works, and He credits His record of righteousness to us. If we're in Him, there's no more work to be done. His yoke is easy, and His burden is light (Matt. 11:30).

WE NEED TO SEE THAT CHRIST ACCOMPLISHED THE WORK WE COULDN'T. ONLY HIS WORK CAN LAST FOREVER.

EVERY CALLING DIGNIFIED

We know this is good news, but sometimes, it doesn't feel very practical. Here are two specific ways the gospel transforms our work in this world: First, when we recognize that we live under the covenant of grace, that Christ has already accomplished everything we need, we'll find, as Luther taught, that "God does not need our good works, but our neighbor does."[26] This allows us to work from a place of rest, knowing that we aren't (and can't) work to earn favor with God. It also dignifies every calling because we recognize that God works through us to meet the needs of His creation:

> *God himself will milk the cows through him whose vocation that is. He who engages in the lowliness of his work performs God's work, be he lad or king. To give one's office proper care is not selfishness. Devotion to office is devotion to love, because it is by God's own ordering that the work of the office is always dedicated to the well-being of one's neighbor. Care for one's office is, in its very frame of reference on earth, participation in God's own care for human beings.[27]*

Second, freed from the burden of making our work give our lives meaning, we'll find that, actually, somehow, it does. Our work is not for merit but for joy. Remember God's mercy in the garden? He could have destroyed Adam and Eve and His fallen creation. But instead, He gives them continued callings through which He will sustain and provide for them. Our vocations become a lens we look through to a God who delights in gifting us with people to love and serve, bodies to use for His glory, and ways to spend our days that turn out to be meaningful in surprising ways. When the Preacher has this realization, he concludes, "I perceived that there is nothing better for them than to be joyful and to do good as long as they live; also that everyone should eat and drink and take pleasure in all his toil—this is God's gift to man" (Eccl. 3:12–13).

Reframing Womanhood

If we want to understand and articulate our purpose as women, we have to start by understanding Genesis on its own terms. We can't pluck out a couple of categories and use them to label all women's work. Neither can we take the original mandate and neglect the progress of redemptive history, the fact that we stand on this side of the mystery of the gospel, revealed in all its fullness. It's unhelpful to strip Genesis of its theological richness to create a career map for ourselves.

So what does the Genesis narrative offer that frames our womanhood if not to declare us solely helpers or child bearers?

Besides showing we are made in God's image, recipients of His mercy, and partners alongside our brothers in the communal work of our earthly and eternal kingdoms, Genesis tells us that God made us female.

We often resist efforts to spell out the differences between men and women, and for good reason. We're prone to over-define them, and now as a society, we're experiencing the whiplash of overcorrection. The fact is, the Bible offers only a few gender-specific commands, which mostly relate to the societal roles each occupy; they don't catalog a list of what is "masculine" or "feminine." We must be careful then not to heap up unnecessary burdens on men and women.

But we're also not just individuals who are distinct from one another.[28] Our sexed differences exist in our bodies and permeate every aspect of who we are. So Blocher—who reminded us that our femaleness will only ever be the second truth about us—writes, "[The woman] does not merely add a few feminine attributes to a 'neutral' humanity. As the hormones permeate the body, so femininity permeates the entire person, intelligence, feeling, and will."[29] Consider the freedom that comes from viewing our differences through this lens of embodiment. As we embrace our male and female bodies, we find freedom for a breadth of personalities, interests, and occupations.

WE'RE NOT CONFINED TO "WOMEN'S WORK," BUT WE DO OUR WORK—AND LIVE OUR LIVES—AS WOMEN.

Author Louise Perry is helpful here, showing us how the differences between men and women exist at the population level and on a bell curve, with outliers on either side. She writes,

> It's very easy to hear "men and women are on average a certain way" and understand this to mean "men and women are always like this," which anyone with any experience of the world will know is not true. There are lots of men and women who are physically dissimilar from other members of their sex, and very many more who don't fit masculine or feminine

stereotypes in terms of their interests and behaviour. In fact, I'd go further, and suggest that almost no one is a walking gender stereotype—I have some stereotypically feminine traits and some stereotypically masculine ones, and I'm sure you do too.

But this kind of anecdotal evidence does not disprove the claim that there are some important average differences between the sexes, and that at the population level these differences have an effect. We can insist simultaneously that there are plenty of exceptions to the rule, and moreover that there is nothing wrong with being an exception to the rule, while also acknowledging the existence of the rule.[30]

The problem comes when we observe these differences and take what ought to be descriptive and make it prescriptive. When we consider what it means to be a woman, we don't need to get overly granular, assigning colors and personality types, career choices and hobbies. But if we're to assert the unique value of women and delight in God's wisdom to make us female, we have to be willing to acknowledge what that entails and consider what faithfulness looks like within its constraints.

We're not confined to "women's work," but we do our work—and live our lives—as women. Convicted that this is a good lot from a wise God who has crafted us in His image to be female, who has redefined us by His mercy, and who has commissioned us with important work to do, let's consider how we live as women—with courage.

PART 2

Courage

5

Vulnerable

ON BEING THE WEAKER VESSEL

They were all slender, frail creatures with wondering eyes and soft fluttery voices. But they were made out of thin invisible steel.

BETTY SMITH, *A TREE GROWS IN BROOKLYN*

When I was in college, my roommate took a self-defense class and invited me to watch her final showcase. As I settled into the small crowd of observers, I wasn't prepared for what a visceral experience it would be. One by one, women entered the arena with a man wearing a large, padded suit. The man would attack them, grabbing from behind or gripping their necks, holding them so they couldn't move. The victim would confidently yell out what she'd learned in class that week as she fought to escape her assailant—"Elbows!" as she jabbed him in his side. "Knees!" as she went for his groin. "Eyeballs!" as she aimed for his most vulnerable points.

For those of us in the crowd, the scenes were more than hypothetical. In the fall of our freshman year, a member of our sorority community was abducted from the mall parking lot after completing a shift at work. Her body was found in the spring; she had been sexually assaulted and brutally murdered.[1] No doubt my roommate and the others enrolled in that self-defense course saw Dru's face—or that of her abductor—as they stared down their own powerlessness. I stood among the spectators, mostly other women, and we watched in stunned silence, choking back tears as we saw a role-play of our deepest fears.

Vulnerable Bodies

Despite our hesitancy to call out specific differences between men and women, facing the reality of that self-defense class requires us to consider the implications of the one major and indisputable difference between men and women—our bodies.

Though it's not without controversy, the fitness and athletic world is one of the few remaining places that generally embraces the physiological differences between men and women. In fact, many scientists and trainers are working hard to expose the problem that, to date, most research related to health and nutrition has been geared toward men, which is doing women a disservice because men and women are not the same. Louise Perry summarizes some of these differences:

> *Adult women are approximately half as strong as adult men in the upper body and two-thirds as strong in the lower body. On average, men can bench press more mass than women can by a factor of roughly two and a half and can punch harder by a similar factor. In hand grip strength, 90 per cent of females produce less force than 95 per cent of males. In other words, almost all women are weaker than almost all men. . . . And men can out-run women, as well as out-punch them.[2]*

I joined a CrossFit gym a couple of years ago and, much to everyone's surprise (including my own), I loved it. I didn't know how good it could feel to lift heavy weights, to push my body to its limit. But no matter how hard I try, I'll never be at the top of the weight lifting leaderboard because I work out with men.

At my gym, every workout-of-the-day has a prescribed level for men and women, varying the weights or reps to match our different physical capacities. Of course, there are exceptions. There are some really strong women who can lift heavier weights than some men, but even they will never beat the strongest men.

When it comes to fitness, it doesn't actually matter that I don't lift the same weight as my male counterparts; what matters is that I push my body to its own limits to achieve maximum gains for my health and well-being. But what about when it comes to life? What are we to make of these physical differences between men and women and what that says about the value and place for women?

Redeeming Vulnerability

Women's physical vulnerability isn't a flaw in creation, it's a result of God's good design of the female body. We've seen that God declared Adam and Eve very good in their sexed bodies. He created men and women to image Him in particular ways, and to use their bodies to do the work He gave them to do.

As they cultivated the land, made a home, nurtured children, or otherwise carried out their functions as prophets, priests, and kings, they would reflect different aspects of God and how He relates to His creation. In their pre-fall state, Eve wouldn't have disdained the vulnerability of her body, and Adam wouldn't have exploited his relative physical strength. Both would have used their bodies for God's glory, delighting in Him as their portion and learning from each other more about God's provision and protection, gentleness and strength.

But what about after the fall? The creation of our sexed bodies is still very good! There's a reason we all think pregnant women glow—the vulnerability of pregnancy is a beautiful thing to behold as a woman turns over her body as a hospitable home for carrying, nurturing, and sustaining new life. But it's not just our potential for childbearing. We'll see in chapter 7 that female sex hormones, which are responsible for our relative weakness compared to men, actually promote relational connectedness, providing stability for societies throughout history. Further, I wonder if it's inherent vulnerability that makes many women more willing and able to express their emotions.

Nonetheless, despite the goodness of God's creation, we also must acknowledge that, in the shadow of sin, women's vulnerability can be a liability, and men's relative strength can be a threat. The apostle Peter affirms this when he speaks into the dynamics of a marriage where a Christian wife is married to an unbelieving husband: "Husbands, live with your wives in an understanding way, showing honor to the woman as the weaker vessel, since they are heirs with you of the grace of life" (1 Peter 3:7).[3] As the "weaker vessel," women are physically vulnerable before their husbands' relative strength, and this would have been especially true in ancient Rome under an unbelieving husband. Louise Perry summarizes it in stark terms: "Natal females experience a permanent physical disadvantage. . . . Almost all men can kill almost all women with their bare hands, but not vice versa."[4]

Given this reality, alongside the lack of recourse available to women facing abuse in the ancient world, Peter commands husbands not to exploit their wives' vulnerability. Godly men will not use their physical strength to wield power over the vulnerable

VULNERABLE

in their midst, and godly women will not view their vulnerability as a reason to cower in the shadows. Instead, Peter points to "the holy women who hoped in God," challenging women to "do good and do not fear anything that is frightening," even as they, in their vulnerability, entrust themselves to one who could do them harm (1 Peter 3:1–6).[5] In other words, Peter calls these weaker vessels to courage.

WHAT IF WEAKER ISN'T WORSE? WHAT IF GOD ACTUALLY HAS A GOOD USE FOR THIS APPARENTLY WEAKER SEX?

God never calls us to bend under sin's distortion; rather, in His kindness, He redeems His fallen image bearers, working to conform us to the image of His Son. His redemptive work takes what the world intends for evil and turns it for our good (see Gen. 50:20). So, if women's vulnerability is part of God's good creation, then I wonder if we should reframe our thinking. What if weaker isn't worse? What if God actually has a good use for this apparently weaker sex? I think the Bible and history testify that He does, and I hope to spend the rest of this chapter persuading you to view your vulnerability as a gift to be stewarded for God's glory.

Vulnerability Leveraged

I don't know if we're allowed to have Bible favorites, but I pick Jehosheba. She's hidden on the pages of 2 Kings, during one of the darkest moments of Israel's history (11:1–3). Both the Northern and Southern kingdoms had descended into wickedness under evil rulers, so God intervenes and brings judgment.[6] He sends a military commander named Jehu to kill both the king of Israel *and* the king of Judah. In Israel, Jehu destroys all the king's descendants and becomes the new ruler. In Judah, Athaliah, mother of the slain king Ahaziah, issues the same command, bent on destroying any

A PLACE FOR YOU

rightful heirs to David's throne so she can seize it for herself.

If you recall the better story of the Bible, the one detailing the battle of two seeds, you'll see in these few chapters a climactic battle. King David's is the line through which God had said He'd bring about His promised deliverer. The evil queen Athaliah stands as the serpent's seed, bent on destroying the promised line once and for all. And it looks like she might succeed.

JEHOSHEBA'S STORY ILLUSTRATES THE OPPORTUNITY EMBEDDED IN WOMEN'S VULNERABILITY.

Except there's a baby. It's Joash, a remaining descendant of King David. And there's Jehosheba, Ahaziah's sister. "But Jehosheba . . . took Joash the son of Ahaziah and stole him away from among the king's sons who were being put to death, and she put him and his nurse in a bedroom. Thus they hid him from Athaliah, so that he was not put to death. And he remained with her six years, hidden in the house of the LORD, while Athaliah reigned over the land" (2 Kings 11:2–3).

Perhaps what I love most about this story is the placement of the word "But." It's how the ESV starts Jehosheba's story—"But Jehosheba . . ." (2 Kings 11:2). This language—"but," "nevertheless," "however"—is the language of the gospel. It shows that what follows is not what's expected. God is breaking in, disrupting the outcome, providing grace. The apostle Paul loves to use this language to communicate the surprising reality of the gospel:

"And you were dead in the trespasses and sins. . . . But God, being rich in mercy . . ." (Eph. 2:1, 4).

"For we ourselves were once foolish, disobedient, led astray . . . But when the goodness and loving kindness of God our Savior appeared, he saved us" (Titus 3:3–5).

"For one will scarcely die for a righteous person—though

VULNERABLE

perhaps for a good person one would dare even to die—*but* God shows his love for us in that while we were still sinners, Christ died for us" (Rom. 5:7–8).

This gospel language is explicit in the New Testament and often implicit in the Old Testament. But we see it in 2 Kings. Jehosheba disrupts the story. She is God's agent of grace.

Jehosheba's story illustrates the opportunity embedded in women's vulnerability. Throughout history, women are invisible, overlooked, and underestimated. Yet their wise stewardship of this status primes them to be used by God to accomplish His redemptive purposes.

Let's consider another example from Scripture. As the book of Exodus opens, Pharaoh is threatened by God's multiplying people, and they are in danger of being wiped out. "Come, let us deal shrewdly with [the Israelites]," he says, "lest they multiply, and, if war breaks out, they join our enemies and fight against us and escape from the land" (Ex. 1:10). He orders the Hebrew midwives to kill the baby boys (Ex. 1:16). Jen Wilkin draws out Pharaoh's implication: "The daughters of Israel are no threat to me."[7]

Let's not forget the significance of the first few chapters of Exodus. This is Moses' origin story, the great deliverer God is going to raise up for His people. He will be a prophet like no other, pointing forward to Christ's work to redeem us from slavery and sin. But first, God's deliverer needs a deliverer. Moses is a baby boy, and there's an order to kill.

As the story continues, God defies the narrative that women are inconsequential. He preserves His people not through one woman but through several—through Shiphrah and Puah, Hebrew midwives who feared God and defied Pharaoh; through Moses' mother, a Levite woman who had faith in God's promises; through Moses' sister Miriam; even through Pharaoh's own daughter (see Ex. 2:1–10).[8] These women's status as weaker vessels made them invisible to Pharaoh, but they were instruments in God's hands. "Israel's first deliverer was not a man in a flowing robe with a streaming beard and a miraculous sign," Jen Wilkin observes. "Israel's first deliverer was a woman in average garb and streaming tears and a miraculous courage."[9]

These aren't isolated stories. Rahab, Jael, Abigail, and Jehoshabeth are just a few examples of Old Testament women who possessed the courage and cunning to become the means through which God protected and provided for His people, preserving the faithful line through whom Christ would come.

AGENTS OF GRACE

In the New Testament, Christ's life and ministry confirm the value of women; He sees and speaks to those whom society deems worthless or invisible (see Mark 5:21–43; Luke 7:36–50; John 4:7–26), and He ensures women have a place among His disciples, including those who stand on their own, without mention of husbands (see Luke 8:1–3; 10:42; Acts 9:36; 16:14).

The Bible tells us that Jesus' disciples fled when He was arrested, while the women stood by Him at the cross (Matt. 26:56; Mark 14:50; John 19:25). We can tend to be hard on these men, and maybe that's fair. Certainly Jesus had prepared them for this moment, foretelling His death and resurrection (Matt. 17:22–23), warning them of coming persecution (John 15:20), and advising them, "Do not fear those who kill the body but cannot kill the soul. Rather fear him who can destroy both soul and body in hell" (Matt. 10:28).

But I wonder if here, too, we can see how God used the women's status as weaker vessels to uniquely position them to be agents of

His grace. In a society that deemed them inconsequential, they could stay by Jesus' side without being considered a threat to the Roman government. They could go to the tomb to anoint Jesus' body while the men remained hidden, and this placed them to be the first eyewitnesses to His resurrection—the ones entrusted by the angel to deliver the good news to the rest of Jesus' disciples (Matt. 28:1, 6–7).

Examples abound in modern history as well. Sonia Purnell's bestselling and award-winning book, *A Woman of No Importance*, tells the story of Virginia Hall, a spy labeled by the Gestapo as "the most dangerous of all Allied spies." Her story is like many women's during wartime—unsuspecting and strategically placed, she seizes the opportunity to wreak havoc on the Nazis while they search frantically for the man causing them problems.

None of this is to suggest that a woman's physical vulnerability is the only asset she offers, the sum of her value and contribution. Rather, these stories illustrate the positional opportunities inherent to our sexes. Think of the places women can go that men cannot, where a man's presence would be seen as a threat, but a woman's presence a welcome comfort. Instead of disdaining our vulnerability, what if we embraced and stewarded the opportunities it affords us? What if our vulnerability actually brings us into the places where we can use all the gifts God has given us, our embodied vulnerability a vessel for God's compassion, wisdom, and insight?

The Essence of Christianity

These stories also invite us to see how God leverages what the world deems weak and inconsequential for His purposes. The Christian paradigm is paradox: strength through weakness; glory through suffering; death, then resurrection. As Christians, we're to embrace this theology of the cross, modeled by Christ Himself (1 Peter 2:23–24). This is the example Peter gives for those who do good but suffer for it (1 Peter 2:20). It's also what grounds his call for wives to submit to their unbelieving husbands, "so that even if some do not obey the word, they may be won without a word by the conduct of their wives, when they see your respectful and pure conduct" (1 Peter 3:1–2).[10] Through the willing sacrifice of One, God brings salvation to many, and this is a pattern we see over and over again.

Mary the mother of Jesus embodies this self-sacrifice as she accepts the Lord's call to bear God's Son: "Behold, I am the servant of the Lord; let it be to me according to your word" (Luke 1:38). "This is what I understand to be the essence of femininity," Elisabeth Elliot writes. "It means surrender."[11] She continues to argue that many aspects of a woman's life require this sort of self-giving.

Those called to marriage or motherhood, Elliot writes, will surrender their independence, names, destinies, wills, bodies—their very lives—for their family's sake.[12] She continues, "The gentle and quiet spirit of which Peter speaks, calling it 'of great worth in God's sight' (1 Peter 3:4), is the true femininity, which found its epitome in Mary, the willingness to be only a vessel, hidden, unknown, except as Somebody's mother. This is the true mother-spirit, true maternity, so absent, it seems to me, in all the annals of feminism."[13]

Elliot is right to highlight these features that are so often inherent to feminine life, reflected not only in marriage and motherhood but in a single life spent devoted to the Lord. But her conclusion is flawed. She observes the value of a woman who makes herself nothing but labels this virtue of pouring out as particularly feminine. Surrender is not the essence of femininity, however; it's the essence of Christianity.

WHAT'S DONE IN SECRET

This surrender ought to characterize every Christian, male or female, but by observing it as a hallmark of feminine life, we can recognize that the church has much to learn from the examples of mothers and grandmothers, sisters and aunts, whose vulnerable position often requires greater sacrifice. When a woman gives over her body to bear and nurture new life, when she sacrifices sleep and strength to care for those entrusted to her, when she risks her life to leverage the position her vulnerability affords her—in each of these ways she models the way of Christ, "who, though he was in the form of God, did not count equality with God a thing to be grasped, but emptied himself, by taking the form of a servant, being born in the likeness of men. And being found in human form, he humbled himself by becoming obedient to the point of death, even death on a cross" (Phil. 2:6–8).

IF WE CONSIDER THE MOST VIBRANT EXAMPLES OF SELF-SACRIFICE IN OUR LIVES, MOST OF US WOULD PROBABLY PICTURE A LINEUP OF WOMEN.

If we all paused for a moment to consider the most vibrant examples of self-sacrifice in our lives, most of us would probably picture a lineup of women, starting with our own mothers. Submission and surrender are not distinctly feminine callings, but they are examples often offered more readily by the women surrounding us, teaching us what it means to heed Christ's call to take up our crosses and follow Him (Matt. 16:24–26). The world might scoff at this, telling women to assert their agency—that is, their ability to exert influence—and throw off the shackles of a life spent in service to others. But the Lord tells us that He sees every deed done in secret, that this way of the cross is the very path to glory. A godly woman indeed has agency, and as she uses it to lay down her life, she finds it. Wise men and women of the church take care to pay attention and learn from her, and to follow her example.

The Perspective of Powerlessness

Scrolling on my Instagram feed recently, I came across a woman's story of walking home late one night. It was dark and shadowy, and she felt anxious and uncomfortable alone on the sidewalk with a man walking toward her. She quickened her pace, probably rehearsed her plan, maybe located her keys or pepper spray, when suddenly she felt the presence of another stranger. She looked over and saw a woman fall into stride beside her. They didn't say anything, just walked together past the man, felt the camaraderie of their vulnerability, the relief of safety in numbers.

It was a sweet story meant to highlight the kindness of a stranger, but it also spoke to me about the inherent sisterhood embedded in a shared experience of being female. As the vulnerable sex, "women understand powerlessness intuitively in a way that men do not," says Jen Wilkin, "[giving] them eyes to see the defenseless, to see the underdog, to see the marginalized in a way that others might not."[14] To illustrate this point, during a talk, Jen highlighted the changes that came about after women were granted the right to vote in the United States:[15]

> *Do you know what has happened in the years that have intervened since [women got the vote]? Things like the Family Medical Leave Act, WIC, better laws against domestic violence. Divorce law was improved so that it wasn't always the husband who got to maintain property or have custody of children. Women's health—all of these issues suddenly came to the table that had never been on the table before.*

Vulnerable

Jen goes on to quote from Jenny Rae Armstrong, who wrote,

During World War I, more American women died in childbirth than American men died on the battlefield. Still, the male legislators didn't see it as an important issue, until the suffragists made it one. In 1921, the suffragists pushed through the Sheppard-Towner act [providing funding for education on prenatal and infant care], and almost overnight, infant and maternal death rates dropped 16% and 12% respectively. By the time those babies were having babies of their own, maternal fatalities were down over 70%, primarily because of women's ability to influence public policy.[16]

It's not that our brothers never experience powerlessness, nor that they can't cultivate eyes to see the defenseless. But the point is that women's perspectives are different and necessary. Our inherent vulnerability acquaints us with powerlessness and, when stewarded well, this becomes a gift to the church, leading to compassion, advocacy, and justice. All Christians are called to care for the least of these, and throughout history, women have led the way in mobilizing the church and society to do it.

It's not just women's experience with and perspective on powerlessness that has the potential to shape the church. Scripture uses the metaphors of labor, birth, nursing, and nurturing to picture the love and care of God for His people. Single women help us to see our eternal state, teaching us about the life of dependence and joy in Christ that awaits. The church is called Christ's bride, and it is God's household, including mothers, daughters, and sisters. This feminine imagery is brought into full color when we're willing to observe and learn from the experiences and perspectives of our sisters.

What About Him?

When we consider the female experience of vulnerability—a life often spent underestimated and overlooked, the endless call to self-sacrifice, the wearying work of advocacy—it's easy to become resentful. It's especially easy to look at our brothers and see all that's unfair. We perceive their strength and agency as delivered on a silver platter while we dodge from street light to street light, trying to feel some semblance of safety. It's no wonder that the women's movement—which, as we saw in the examples above was needed—has become what it is today, moving from good advocacy for the marginalized to loud self-assertion, demanding unrestricted equal treatment. Exploring these things could be a book all on its own, but I want to offer a few thoughts for how we can courageously navigate these struggles as women of conviction.

> **CHRISTIAN MEN AND WOMEN ARE BOTH CALLED TO LAY DOWN THEIR LIVES FOR THE SAKE OF CHRIST AND NEIGHBOR.**

INTENDED FOR MUTUAL FLOURISHING

First, I think we need to acknowledge how the differences between men and women have been over-defined throughout history, both outside the church and within it. We have taken the physiological differences God intended for our mutual flourishing, and we have made them into prisons for one another. Our sex does not dictate who should do the dishes or change the diapers; it doesn't create particular career paths or relegate personality traits as masculine or feminine. The reality is, Christian men and women are both called to lay down their lives for the sake of Christ and neighbor, and how this looks will vary based on demeanor and background, season and circumstance.

VULNERABLE

Second, we need to acknowledge the way sin can cause these differences between men and women to lead to oppressive power dynamics, resulting in the exclusion of women from places of influence, dismissiveness toward our perspectives, or even exploitation and abuse. Because of this, despite the clarion calls of modern feminists, I think we need something better to advocate for than equality.

If men and women are different, how can the same set of rules serve both of our interests? The sexual revolution peddled this lie, telling women we could experience the same sexual freedom as men. This could never be true for a number of reasons, but especially because men can never get pregnant. So this sexual freedom will always cost a woman more, whether through bearing the hormonal toll of birth control, the emotional and physical toll of an abortion, or the total life upheaval of an unplanned pregnancy (and/or a shotgun wedding).[17] "We in the West are, perhaps, liberated enough," journalist Mary Harrington argues, "but we have not given enough thought to the differences between men and women's interests, shaped by our embodied realities.[18]

This might seem like a leap from our present discussion—I doubt many of you are reading this chapter to claim your rights from the sexual revolution. But I think it's important to observe the foundation of the argument for women's equality. It aims to defy the differences between men and women, to flatten and neutralize them, and this ultimately doesn't serve women. We need to think deeply before making one-size-fits-all proclamations. Louise Perry suggests that we're asking the wrong questions. Instead of trying to figure out what equal freedoms look like, we need to consider how we might invest in the flourishing of both men and women, acknowledging that we have different interests.[19] I am deeply concerned about women's freedom and flourishing, but

113

like Harrington and Perry, I've come to question if equality is the right category for us. And, if I'm honest, I'm hard-pressed to consider it a biblical one.

> **IN WHATEVER CIRCUMSTANCE, JESUS SAYS, "YOU FOLLOW ME." AND HE SAYS THIS IS THE WAY OF BLESSING.**

Which brings me to one more thing. At the end of John's gospel, Jesus tells Peter that he's going to die for Christ's sake:

> *"Truly, truly, I say to you, when you were young, you used to dress yourself and walk wherever you wanted, but when you are old, you will stretch out your hands, and another will dress you and carry you where you do not want to go." (This he said to show by what kind of death he was to glorify God.) And after saying this he said to him, "Follow me." (John 21:18–19)*

In true Peter fashion, he looks around and sees John and asks, "Lord, what about this man?" (v. 21). Jesus replies, "If it is my will that he remain until I come, what is that to you? You follow me!" (v. 22).

What if Jesus has called you to a life of pouring out for His sake? What if it never feels like the men around you are called to the same sacrifice? What if you spend your life on behalf of the oppressed and no one ever notices? What if you never feel like your perspective is valued? In each case, Jesus says, "You follow Me."

And He says this is the way of blessing.

NOT AN AFTERTHOUGHT

It grieves me to think of how much the church loses when it ignores the strategic placement, godly examples, and wise perspectives of the women in its midst. But it also grieves me to

VULNERABLE

think of the ways we rob ourselves of the joy of serving Christ because we become so consumed with fighting to be seen and heard that we miss the good works God has set before us. I'm not suggesting we don't take up the work of advocacy, that we don't continue to pray for the church to seek the flourishing of both men and women, that we don't plead with our brothers to lend us their agency, to value the daughters, sisters, aunts, moms, and grandmas in their midst.

But when I consider examples from the Bible and history, I can only conclude that we are surrounded by a great cloud of witnesses—godly women who feared the Lord and not men, who didn't wait to get a man's permission or his acknowledgment, who faithfully stewarded the opportunities God entrusted to them. The place for you is, at least in part, the place where you are. Sisters, let us run the race set before us, believing that "[our] Father who sees in secret will reward [us]" (Matt. 6:4). He promises that the humble will be exalted at the proper time (1 Peter 5:6), that no matter how wearying the work, God himself will "restore, confirm, strengthen, and establish" us (v. 10). Jen Wilkin says,

> We fear God more than Pharaoh. We link arms with one another. We nurture life in the face of death. We intercede bravely on behalf of the helpless, the voiceless, the marginalized, and we deliver the kingdom with trembling hands. This is our role. It is not a sideline role. It is not a role of weakness. It is a role that will require every ounce of courage that you have. Women, daughters, sisters, you are not an afterthought. What you bring to the body of Christ, to the mission of the church, is not of secondary importance.... You have eyes that see the helpless and the marginalized. You have hands that reach to the forgotten and the outcast.

You have a heart that beats for the defenseless. Use your smarts, use your empathy, use your bravery and every ounce of your physical strength to nurture life in the face of death.[20]

Clothed with Strength and Dignity

Raising daughters, I often come back to that self-defense class. I wonder how to teach my daughters to see that their vulnerability doesn't undermine their agency, that their powerlessness may shape their perspective, cultivating compassion for others, but it need not paralyze them. Being vulnerable doesn't mean embracing weakness in a way that leads to victimhood or passivity. It doesn't mean we don't work to build strength, or even take a self-defense class. There's a reason I work out: I want to be ready for whatever God calls me to in service of Him.

WE WEAKER VESSELS CAN STILL WORK TO CULTIVATE PHYSICAL, EMOTIONAL, AND MENTAL STRENGTH FOR THE LIVES GOD HAS GIVEN TO US.

On a recent beach day, my son was wading in the water while we all sat far up on the shore. Suddenly, I heard him calling out, and as I looked up, I couldn't tell what was wrong, but I knew he was distressed and stuck in the water. I sprinted to the shore, plowed through the waves, picked him up, and carried him out of the water, blood dripping from his ankle from being stung by a stingray. I confess, for a moment, I felt like superwoman, like I could have carried that boy wherever he needed to go. I felt grateful for my strong body, my maternal response—my ability to offer nurture and comfort while also possessing the strength needed to handle the crisis.

Not all of us have the ability to build physical strength, I know.

You may be plagued by chronic illness or pain, by injury or other limitations, or maybe you simply share my allergy to running. This makes you no less of a woman. My point is not to heap a new burden of CrossFit training on you; my point is that we weaker vessels can still work to cultivate physical, emotional, and mental strength for the lives God has given to us, even as we lean on him in our weakness.

The Proverbs 31 woman has been weaponized and misapplied in ways that make her feel like a crushing weight, but I think that's a shame. This paragon of feminine virtue—and embodiment of Lady Wisdom herself—is pictured as a worker. She is clothed with both strength and dignity (Prov. 31:25). "She dresses herself with strength and makes her arms strong" (v.17). She has cultivated her vulnerable body in such a way that she is fit for the tasks God has called her to. Over the course of her lifetime, (and I think this chapter describes the span of her seasons, not a day in her life) she has the energy to last through a day of hard labor; she has diverse skills and interests; she cares for her household and engages in business; she has a sweet marriage and relationship with her children. I appreciate how the passage shows that she uses her body in service to her callings; she doesn't just have a great personality.

Yet, at the end of the day, it's her fear of the Lord that causes her praise (v. 30).

We can only make our bodies so strong, but I think that's why the Bible gives us this call to cultivate inner beauty. We may have soft bodies, weak arms, and fragile necks, but if we are women who fear the Lord, we can be made of thin invisible steel. Our vulnerability gives us a unique path to resilience. In our weakness, God's strength is made perfect, and we get to experience firsthand the delight of depending on Him.

6

Quiet

ON FINDING YOUR VOICE

"I like good strong words, that mean something."

JO MARCH, *LITTLE WOMEN*

In the now-a-bit-cringe 1999 rom-com *Never Been Kissed*, Drew Barrymore's nerdy childhood character gets asked to the prom. In her excitement, she says, "I'm actually speechless! I have no words! That's never happened to me! Words are my life!" Despite the devastating moment we know will come when she finds out the invitation was a cruel joke, this is one of my favorite movie lines.

I'm a verbal processor who's always been bursting at the seams with ideas, ready to work them out with anyone willing to listen. It's a rare moment that I would be short on words. I'd like to think this is one of my more endearing qualities, of course. I'm good at making conversation, helping to direct the discussion to big ideas or deep reflections. But every time I leave a social gathering, insecurity settles as a pit in my stomach. Without fail, I turn to my husband on the drive home and ask, "Did I talk too much?"

Given my propensity to word vomit in contrast to my introverted husband, and my experience on the listening end of my similarly verbose children, two of whom are daughters, I've always assumed it's true that women are the more verbal sex. When I originally planned this chapter, I expected to start with this statement of fact about another difference between men and women rooted in God's design of the sexes. But what I found instead is that the statistics suggesting women speak more than men have been debunked.[1] In fact, across numerous studies, the difference in the volume of words between boys and girls is negligible.[2] Linguist Deborah Tannen observes differences between the speech patterns of men and women, but she attributes them to context: Women tend to talk more in the context of friendship—in private settings—while men tend to dominate public spaces, like workplaces.[3]

Reviewing these studies is a bit like that moment in *The Sixth Sense* when you realize you had it all wrong, where every scene replays and you see it clearly for the first time. Tannen's work demonstrates what I have experienced in my own life: Women are generally more cautious about their words, especially in public settings. Concerned about avoiding the negative labels of bossy, aggressive, or self-promoting, they work to downplay their strengths to "save face" for others.[4] In other words, aware of the negative stereotypes gunning for them, women "try to take up less verbal space," Tannen writes.[5] Although men and women both speak an average of 16,000 words per day, women spend a lot of time worried they've said too much.[6]

Aren't You Supposed to Be Quiet?

Somewhere along the way, I've internalized the idea that women are supposed to be quiet, even if I've always been a little bad at it.

Quietness as a feminine virtue has a long history. In *Ever After,* another Drew Barrymore gem that reimagines the classic Cinderella story, Jacqueline—the less unpleasant stepsister—expresses an idea about women's voices that has persisted through the ages: "A lady of breeding ought never to raise her voice any louder . . ." she drops her voice, so that it's barely heard, ". . . than the gentle hum of a whispering wind."

What I find today, however, is less talk about women's need for quietness, and more about the female need to reclaim her voice. This feminist rallying cry was summarized well in 2017 when the phrase "Nevertheless, She Persisted" took the mainstage.[7] These words were spoken in frustration by Senator Mitch McConnell after Senator Elizabeth Warren continued her speech on the Senate floor, despite a vote that should have muted her: "Senator Warren was giving a lengthy speech. . . . She had appeared to violate the rule. She was warned. She was given an explanation. Nevertheless, she persisted."[8]

McConnell's phrase had unintended consequences, sparking a movement of women weary of being silenced. As one woman said, "'Nevertheless, She Persisted' is really about every woman who really had to use her tenacity and courage to accomplish whatever she set out to accomplish. It's universal. . . . You think about our mothers and grandmothers—they've been persisting for a very long time."[9]

Regardless of the original context of Warren's speech, I can see why the phrase has become a source of inspiration, representing women who have had to overcome innumerable obstacles for their voices to be heard. I feel some semblance of kinship, knowing what it's like to feel silenced, to watch men shift in their seats in discomfort as I ask questions or share ideas. I know the sinking feeling of wanting to use my voice to stop an unwanted advance, to advocate for myself or others, but feeling like I'm supposed to just quietly accept what's coming. And I know the nausea that accompanies the fear that I have overshared. For all the words I speak in a day, it's taken a lot of my adult life to learn how to speak *up*.

Nonetheless, the notion that women are to be quiet appears to be, well, biblical. So we find ourselves in a bit of a conundrum. Perhaps we feel the words caught up in our throats. We know we have perspective and insight to offer, but we fear speaking where our voices are not welcomed. Thus we're poised to be sympathetic to a world beckoning us to be loud. Yet we also know how the Bible speaks about words, the power of the tongue to burn everything (and everyone) down (see James 3:6–8). "When words are many, transgression is not lacking," the wise man tells us, "but whoever restrains his lips is prudent" (Prov. 10:19). So we long to be women who use our tongues to prevent, not cause, forest fires (James 3:5), who can win people over "without a word" (1 Peter 3:1).

At the end of the day, I want to know what it looks like to steward my voice. Where is the place for my perspective? In what spaces will my voice be heard, and what do I do about the spaces where it won't? And what does it look like for me to speak—or not—with courage?

When the Bible Silences Women

We can point to a few key Bible passages where women are told to be quiet. Since these texts often cause us to bristle, I think it's worth making some observations about the context and interpretation of each one and then situating these gender-specific commands within the broader scope of Scripture and God's instruction for His people about the wise use of words.

LET THEM LEARN!

Let's start with what I think are the hardest passages to swallow. In 1 Corinthians 14:33–35, the apostle Paul writes, "As in all the churches of the saints, the women should keep silent in the churches. For they are not permitted to speak, but should be in submission, as the Law also says. If there is anything they desire to learn, let them ask their husbands at home. For it is shameful for a woman to speak in church." I'm going to pair this one with Paul's similar teaching in 1 Timothy 2:11–12: "Let a woman learn quietly with all submissiveness. I do not permit a woman to teach or to exercise authority over a man; rather, she is to remain quiet."

Since we tend to focus on what's being restricted here, it's worth noting first what's being commended. The women are learning! They're present, included in the church's gathered worship. This itself was countercultural in a time and place where women's assumed mental inferiority often resulted in a lack of education and exclusion from spaces reserved for discussing ideas and making decisions.[10] Like Jesus who affirmed Mary sitting in the disciples' place of learning at His feet (Luke 10:42), Paul commends women's belonging, saying, "Let a woman learn!"

DIG IN!

What was it like for women to be welcomed into these spaces? My modern, Western orientation can't fathom being restricted from going to school, learning to read, or engaging in thoughtful dialogue. But in the church, many women grow up believing that studying doctrine is for men. In my experience of learning alongside these women, it's like watching the lights come on. There's something invigorating about digging deeply into the Scriptures for the first time. Suddenly encouraged to love God with our minds, we find that our minds can't get enough. We've encountered the depths of the riches of the wisdom of God, and we've got questions.

It reminds me of that stage in my children's development when they start learning to read. The whole world comes to life before them, and now they want to read everything aloud—every billboard, every book page, every slide behind the pastor as he preaches. In their eagerness, they overflow with words and questions, trying to piece together a word-filled world that has thus far been kept out of reach. It's wonderful, but it's noisy. And part of awakening to this process of learning is also developing intuition for when to speak—and when not to.

PAUL DOESN'T RESTRICT WOMEN'S CONTRIBUTION WHOLESALE; HE HAS A PARTICULAR CONTEXT IN MIND.

It makes sense, then, that Paul follows his affirmation of women's learning with some guidance about how they should engage in these public settings, suggests a denominational report on the role of women in ministry. "Since no one can learn if noisy and insubordinate," the report says, "it is sensible that Paul would request women to learn quietly, which is an indication of their submission."[11] Quietness shows a student's receptivity to teaching and awareness of the proper time and place for questions. It also shows the student understands his or her role in the gathered assembly. In Paul's time, this was a new experience for women, and he offers guidance for engaging properly and respectfully.

ALL THINGS IN ORDER

Paul doesn't tell only women to be silent; in that same passage he restricts members from speaking in other contexts to prevent chaos (1 Cor. 14:26–33). He also describes women speaking among God's people elsewhere and, rather than rebuke them, he

QUIET

gives instructions for when they pray and prophesy, and notes that various members (male and female) bring to worship "a hymn, a lesson, a revelation, a tongue, or an interpretation" (1 Cor. 11:5; 14:26). So, he's not restricting women's contribution wholesale; he has a particular context in mind.[12] The same is true in 1 Timothy, where Paul is speaking about the authoritative ruling and teaching functions of the office of pastor/elder.[13]

Paul's aim is not to silence women broadly; he's concerned about order (1 Cor. 14:40; 1 Tim. 3:14–15). In the context of these passages, there were specific cases where women needed guidance on the proper time to speak. But, in general, this need for order includes how we relate as men and women, but also as officers and laypeople (1 Tim. 2:8–3:13), participants in gathered worship (1 Cor. 14:26–40), members of Christ's body offering various gifts for mutually building one another up (1 Cor. 12), and siblings living alongside one another in God's family (1 Tim. 3:14–15; 5:2).

Further, though his instruction for women to be silent is jarring to our modern ears, the Greek word Paul chooses in 1 Corinthians 14 doesn't restrict speech altogether. "It can mean to keep something to oneself (Luke 9:36), to listen (Acts 15:12), or to be silent after speaking (Luke 20:26; Act 15:13)."[14] Its earlier uses in the same passage clearly mean the speaker will pause their speaking to let others have a turn.[15] The same is true for the word used in 1 Timothy 2:12: "[It] can mean total silence, but more often describes a quiet attitude. . . . [This] term seems apt to describe the relative silence that is a virtue for students."[16]

A HEART POSTURE

Ultimately, Paul's instructions for women to be silent are aimed at the heart, calling us to adopt a humble posture of learning while yielding to the authority of church officers "so that all may learn and all be encouraged" (1 Cor. 14:31). In 1 Corinthians and 1 Timothy, Paul comments on contexts specifically pertaining to women, likely in part because of the particular circumstances of the early church. I'm persuaded that aspects of Paul's gender-specific instructions transcend the time and place of his writing, which we'll consider further when we look at his instructions about church officers, but I don't think we can argue his commands to be quiet are somehow targeting the female nature. His instructions apply to all church members in various contexts and are given elsewhere to the church more broadly.

Humbly accepting instruction is the pathway to wisdom (see Prov. 19:20). And, in Hebrews, all Christians are told, "Obey your leaders and submit to them, for they are keeping watch over your souls, as those who will have to give an account" (Heb. 13:17). Overall, these passages aren't about the absolute silence of women but a posture of learning that maintains order, a call placed upon all God's people.

The Power of Silence

Let's look at another one. Peter instructs wives: "Be subject to your own husbands, so that even if some do not obey the word, they may be won without a word by the conduct of their wives, when they see your respectful and pure conduct" (1 Peter 3:1–2). He then goes on to issue what seems like a broader command relevant to all women: "Let your adorning be the hidden person of the heart with the imperishable beauty of a gentle and quiet spirit, which in God's sight is very precious" (1 Peter 3:4).

Though this passage seems to silence women, here too it's important to observe how it actually affirms their agency or influence. Peter writes to wives whose husbands may be unbelievers, which means these women have come to (or remained in their) faith *apart* from their husbands. This means they have heard the gospel, put their faith in Christ, and joined the church of their own volition. This was a consistent story in the early church and throughout the ages. Women flocked to Christianity, often without their husbands.[17] These early converts likely took to heart Paul's encouragement to stay in their challenging—and often dangerous circumstances— persisting in prayer that, through their witness, God would save their husbands (1 Cor. 7:12–16). And often, He did. Historian Rodney Stark observes how these conversions affected whole households and brought Christianity into the wealthy and powerful corners of society, often resulting in protection for the church and persecuted Christians.[18]

This information about the early church could also explain why Peter speaks first to the wives of unbelieving husbands. Not because women in particular ought to speak less, as we'll see, but simply because many women found themselves in these circumstances.

IN CHALLENGING SITUATIONS

Have you ever sat with a woman whose husband is an unbeliever? Whether she has come to faith without him or he has departed from his faith since they married, the burden she carries is heavy. She loves this man, but she grieves for him. There's a distance between them that can't be overcome apart from Christ's work in her husband's heart, which means she often feels lonely, helpless, and discouraged. Maybe she has pleaded with him, using her words to try to convince him of the truth, goodness, and beauty of the gospel. But nothing she says seems to make a difference.

Think of how Peter's words would have encouraged this

woman. He tells wives they are doing God's work, imitating their Savior who, "when he was reviled, he did not revile in return; when he suffered, he did not threaten, but continued entrusting himself to him who judges justly" (1 Peter 2:23). *Your conduct is powerful*, he says. *When you entrust yourself to Christ and sacrificially love and respect your husband, you become a window through which your husband can see Jesus.*

He then turns to the whole church, weary of doing good in a culture that hates them simply for their affiliation with Jesus. Among this letter's recipients are doubtless members who have lost spouses and siblings, parents and dear friends over their conversion to Christianity. They long for these loved ones to know life in Christ. They long for their suffering to be worth something. And Peter tells them it is. As they honor Christ in their hearts and go about their lives, people will ask the reason for the hope within them (1 Peter 3:15).

> **WORDS ARE POWERFUL, BUT SOMETIMES THEY FALL ON DEAF EARS. OUR SILENCE CAN BE POWERFUL TOO.**

STRATEGIC SILENCE

I've often read this passage as a rebuke. "You're not your husband's Holy Spirit," we say to one another, and it's true. I'm often guilty of trying to use my words to control and manipulate others, arrogantly convinced I know what's best for them. But there's a reason Proverbs likens a nagging wife to a dripping faucet (Prov. 27:15). It's not only annoying; eventually, it becomes white noise.

In a sense, then, Peter is indeed commending silence, both to these wives and to the church at large. But their silence is strategic. It may ultimately create opportunities for speech. This is how God drew us to Himself, and it's how He continues to build

QUIET

His church—through the quiet work of His Spirit preparing our hearts for a well-timed word, the faithful proclamation of the gospel (Prov. 15:23; Rom. 10:17).

We know words are powerful, but sometimes they fall on deaf ears. Peter's encouragement is that our silence can be powerful too. In these quiet places, God is still working.

Perhaps this is why Peter turns next to the gentle and quiet spirit "which in God's sight is very precious" (1 Peter 3:4). This isn't the demeanor of a doormat who has been robbed of her voice, but rather the disposition of one whose heart is in order because she fears the Lord.

This is quietness to which we all—male and female—ought to aspire. The word Peter uses for "quiet" is the same Paul uses in 1 Timothy 2, not when he refers to women but to the whole church: "First of all, then, I urge that supplications, prayers, intercessions, and thanksgivings be made for all people, for kings and all who are in high positions, that we may lead a peaceful and *quiet* life, godly and dignified in every way" (1 Tim. 2:1–2).

Peter commends a similar quiet godliness to the whole church: "Finally, all of you, have unity of mind, sympathy, brotherly love, a tender heart, and a humble mind. Do not repay evil for evil or reviling for reviling, but on the contrary, bless, for to this you were called, that you may obtain a blessing" (1 Peter 3:8–9). He goes on to quote from Psalm 34, describing the life of righteousness that befits all Christians: "Let him keep his tongue from evil and his lips from speaking deceit; let him turn away from evil and do good; let him seek peace and pursue it" (1 Peter 3:10–11).

This is quietness found in repentance and rest, stillness and trust (Isa. 30:15). It's quietness that comes as we are stilled and settled in the love of God (Zeph. 3:17). The psalmist describes it as steadiness:

> For the righteous will never be moved;
> he will be remembered forever.
> He is not afraid of bad news;
> his heart is firm, trusting in the LORD.
> His heart is steady; he will not be afraid,
> until he looks in triumph on his adversaries. (Ps. 112:6–8)

NOT ONLY FOR WOMEN

So why does Peter specifically tell women to cultivate a gentle and quiet spirit? He contrasts inner beauty with external adornment, presumably because women of the age were more tempted than men to dress and style their hair extravagantly to draw attention to their wealth or status. This squares with Stark's observations about the high number of wealthy women who converted to Christianity. Perhaps Peter has their discipleship in mind.

Might we also see some broad, gender-specific tendencies that persist today? Though we balk at stereotypes (and often rightly so), it's likely still fair to say broadly (and not without exception) that women are more tempted than men to leverage their external beauty and sexual appeal. Paul addresses this female tendency as well, cautioning women to dress themselves with good works, not external adornment (1 Tim. 2:9–10). Overly fixating on external adornment is *loud*, striving for attention, status, and opportunities.

But Peter and Paul are not suggesting women are the only ones with sin to fight against. In both passages, they turn immediately to some stereotypical masculine struggles. Peter challenges men not to exploit their relative strength and mistreat their wives, but rather to live with their wives in an understanding way (1 Peter 3:7). And Paul warns them against anger and quarreling (1 Tim.

2:8). We could argue that implicit to both warnings is an admonition about the wise use of words.

The Wise Woman Builds Her House

At the end of the day, the Bible doesn't silence women—it quiets us all. And, as we observed about surrender in the last chapter, the wise stewardship of words isn't a feminine calling but a Christian one. Yet, also like surrender, our placement and perspective as females offer unique opportunities to use our words to build up—or tear down. We saw in our review of Genesis how the story of the fall testifies to women's tremendous influence.[19] Perhaps this is why Proverbs uses feminine imagery to depict both Lady Wisdom and Lady Folly. Their presence in the Scriptures confronts the claims that the Bible aims to silence women, presenting instead a beautiful model of restrained, godly speech.

Let's observe a few things about these two literary figures. First, these metaphors are *both* women. The writer doesn't juxtapose "Lady Folly" with "Sir Wisdom." This is personification, of course, a literary device to help us picture and internalize the lesson. But imagery is effective because it draws on our real-life experiences. The Sage is counting on our experience of both wise and foolish women to illustrate his point.

Second, wisdom is a woman, but *she still speaks*. Lady Folly is loud, using her words to ensnare fellow fools (Prov. 9:13–18). But Lady Wisdom also "cries aloud in the street" (Prov. 1:20). Look at how much her wisdom is expressed through words:

Does not wisdom call?

Does not understanding raise her voice?

On the heights beside the way,

at the crossroads she takes her stand;

beside the gates in front of the town,

at the entrance of the portals she cries aloud:
"To you, O men, I call,
and my cry is to the children of man.
O simple ones, learn prudence;
O fools, learn sense.
Hear, for I will speak noble things,
and from my lips will come what is right,
for my mouth will utter truth;
wickedness is an abomination to my lips.
All the words of my mouth are righteous;
there is nothing twisted or crooked in them.
They are all straight to him who understands,
and right to those who find knowledge.
Take my instruction instead of silver,
and knowledge rather than choice gold,
for wisdom is better than jewels,
and all that you may desire cannot compare with her.
(Prov. 8:1–11)

In fact, in unpacking the way of wisdom, the book of Proverbs offers at least forty maxims related to the way we do (or do not) speak. When the Sage writes, "The wisest of women builds her house, but folly with her own hands tears it down (Prov. 14:1), he likely has in mind the woman who "opens her mouth with wisdom, and the teaching of kindness is on her tongue" (Prov. 31:26), in contrast to the one by whose mouth a city is overthrown (Prov. 11:11).

CHRIST, THE WISDOM OF GOD

Finally, Lady Wisdom ultimately depicts and points to Christ, "the wisdom of God" (1 Cor. 1:24). This blesses me on multiple fronts. The most important of which is that Jesus has no qualms about this feminine imagery helping us see His purpose and character. The voice of Wisdom crying out in the streets evokes the voice of Jesus, calling us to follow Him.

Maybe it's because of Lady Wisdom that this voice crying out makes me think of my childhood days at my grandparents' farm. We would scatter into the far corners of their property with our cousins for hours, climbing hay bales or riding snowmobiles, building forts or exploring barns. My grandma had an old metal bell in her backyard, and when we heard that bell ring, we knew it was time to come in. Probably hot food was waiting, and in the winters, mugs of cocoa or Russian tea. The bell—a symbol of my mom, grandma, and aunts beckoning us home—gathered us, warmed us, and reset us. Unashamedly, Jesus claims this imagery for Himself, likening Himself to a mother hen gathering her chicks (Luke 13:34).

Here's another reason to love how Lady Wisdom points to Jesus: Our emphasis on quieting women implies some inherent feminine capacity to tame our tongues. But "no human being can tame the tongue," James tells us. "It is a restless evil, full of deadly poison" (James 3:8). I know this all too well, often using my words like a sword instead of an instrument of healing (Prov. 12:18). The Bible testifies to the ways foolish women can use their words to lead people astray, and I know my own capacity for being a foolish counselor. But this relationship between Lady Wisdom and Jesus relieves the pressure I feel to live up to Lady Wisdom's example. I can't. But I'm supposed to look through Lady Wisdom onto Christ. Only He can tame the tongue. We need His perfect words to speak for us, His record of righteousness covering every reckless word we've spoken. Only in the words spoken over us by the Word made flesh will we ultimately find life (John 1:1, 4; Prov. 8:35).

And last, though no human being can tame the tongue, we're united to wisdom personified and indwelt by His Spirit. We are not mere mortals. Lady Wisdom points us to Christ's work *for* us, but also *in* and *through* us. By God's grace, we can become women whose words offer life, comfort, and wisdom. We can learn when to be quiet and when to speak the truth in love to build others up, giving grace to all who hear (Eph. 4:15, 29).

Words Are Our Life

"Out of the abundance of the heart his mouth speaks," Jesus taught (Luke 6:45), reminding us that we don't speak to pile up words but to reflect God's heart. And to do that, we must be saturated with God's Word. Words are our life! As the word of Christ dwells in us richly, we become those who teach and admonish one another in all wisdom (Col. 3:16). The Bible offers numerous examples for what it looks like for women to be shaped by God's Word and steward their voices.

Miriam, Huldah, and Deborah served Israel as prophetesses, raised up by God to "interpret events and lead Israel's response to it" (see Ex. 15; 2 Kings 21–22; Judg. 4).[20] Women provided wise counsel, such as Queen Esther, who convinced a pagan king to act in justice and thus kept the Jews in Persia from being destroyed (Est. 4–8). Likewise, Abigail's speech to David in 1 Samuel displays her incredible wisdom; her words keep David from the guilt of bloodshed (1 Sam. 25:23–31). This is a characteristic of the Proverbs 31 woman, who is a trusted confidante and counselor of her husband (Prov. 31:11–12).

We've observed how Jesus, and later Paul, affirmed women's roles as disciples. Women are also noted to be teachers, like Priscilla who, alongside her husband Aquila, pulled Apollos aside and "explained to him the way of God more accurately" (Acts 18:26). Paul credits Timothy's faith to the persistent instruction of his mother and grandmother, Lois and Eunice (2 Tim. 1:5). And in Titus, Paul calls the older women to teach the younger women what is good as they model godliness rooted in sound doctrine (Titus 2:3–5).

Women are also noted encouragers. I think of how the Proverbs 31 woman embodies wisdom; she's described as having "the teaching of kindness" on her tongue (Prov. 31:26). Women stood by Jesus' side at His crucifixion (John 19:25), and Paul describes one woman as being like a mother to him (Rom. 16:13).

The Bible records rich theological content from the mouths of women, including prayers from Hannah (1 Sam. 2:1–10) and Mary (Luke 1:46–55), and Martha's declaration of Jesus' identity: "Yes, Lord; I believe that you are the Christ, the Son of God, who is coming into the world" (John 11:27). The woman at the well evangelizes her community after her encounter with Christ (John 4:29, 39). Women are also the first heralds after Christ's resurrection (Luke 24:10).

The Place For Your Voice

Despite the plethora of biblical examples of wise female voices, and the others we can point to throughout history and as we survey our own lives, you might still feel silenced. You might still *be* silenced for a number of reasons. Studies document different speech patterns for men and women and, while women have their own vices, stereotypes about negative male verbal behavior like mansplaining, interrupting, dominating meetings, and taking credit for their female coworkers' ideas are well-founded.[21] Women whose work consistently places them in these kinds of environments may have to wrestle through what it looks like to walk the path of self-advocacy or surrender, with patience, humility, and wisdom.

In complementarian churches where qualified men hold the office of pastor/elder, we may feel like our voices aren't valued and our perspectives dismissed. Jesus and Paul both provide examples to male leaders of what it looks like to view sisters as partners in the gospel, doing ministry side by side. Welcoming female perspectives doesn't mean relinquishing leadership. Pastors can seek the counsel of wise and godly women even as these qualified men bear responsibility for whatever the outcome is. But in the church, too, God calls His daughters to wisdom. There's "a time to keep silence, and a time to speak" the Preacher of Ecclesiastes tells us (Eccl. 3:7), and it takes wisdom to discern which is which.

WELCOMING FEMALE PERSPECTIVES DOESN'T MEAN RELINQUISHING LEADERSHIP.

The world tells us to be loud, to persist, to raise our voices and demand to be heard. But this sounds a lot like Lady Folly's call. And it's ultimately rooted in fear. We fear if we are not heard, we are not valued. We fear if our perspective is not included, we will lose control. We fear being obsolete, invisible, ordinary. We fear what people will think of us if we speak up, and if we don't.

But Lady Wisdom calls us to a different fear—the fear of the Lord. This, she says, is the beginning of wisdom (Prov. 9:10). This quiets us, sets us to repenting, trusting, resting, listening. In these spaces where it feels like our voices are not valued, where we feel invisible and silenced, we can be reminded that God not only sees us, He also hears us (Gen. 16:11–13). How many words go unrecorded, whispered prayers on the lips of God's daughters? These words are like incense, a pleasing aroma to the Lord (Rev. 5:8; 8:3–4). With a quieted heart before the Lord, our prayers offered to Him, we find He provides the wisdom to know when to speak and the courage to trust Him to do with our words whatever He wills.

7

Limited

ON THE DIGNITY OF BEING HUMAN (AND THE JOY OF FORMING A VILLAGE)

> *"Give it to your sister, it doesn't hurt, and*
> *See if she can handle every family burden*
> *Watch as she buckles and bends but never breaks,*
> *no mistakes"*
>
> LUISA MADRIGAL, *ENCANTO*

I started writing this chapter after spending most of the day in bed, unable to breathe through my nose. Facing my third bout of sickness in six weeks, I'm also staring down this book deadline, which has already required one extension and now falls right at the end of my children's Christmas break, which comes after a week of hosting my in-laws, which comes after Christmas (and all the preparation that requires), which comes after a water leak that led to an unexpected kitchen and living room remodel. They say when it rains, it pours, and I can attest that it's true, and that it's particularly unfortunate when the rain is happening in the unseen space behind your fridge, and you don't discover it until it seeps through your living room floors.

In seasons like this, I walk around in that liminal space between laughing and crying, waiting for the next thing to break.

Actually, I live in that space. This is just another day in the Dahl house.

The Quest to Be Invincible

I'm one of those women who wants to do all the things, and I always have been. In fact, it's still a sore spot with my siblings that my mom let me take "mental health days" in high school. But it's not that I was favored, it's that it made my mom tired just to look at me. So when I asked if I could skip the part where I pretend to be sick and just stay home and rest, she responded with "yes, please."

People are always trying to convince me I don't need to do so much. They worry I'm driven by a fearful need to please. Surely, there have been stretches where my motives are messed up, where I'm running myself ragged to prove something, like that time I thought we should do foster care while having two toddlers and a preschooler of our own. But, in general, I insist that I'm grateful for everything on my plate; I just wish sometimes my plate were a little bigger so things would stop falling off.

It's a delight to do my work, both inside and outside my home, but if I'm honest, I often keep a tight grip on my responsibilities and a tight lid on my struggles to manage them all, fearing any admission of diminished capacity will mean I have to give something up—or it will be taken from me. So instead, I believe I'm invincible, that I can do everything simply because I want to. Unfortunately, my sinuses beg to differ. Sickness has this way of inconveniently forcing me to look at my humanity head-on, to acknowledge how tired I actually am, to make me rest.

LIMITED

In these moments of pause, I sometimes discover resentment that has been boiling beneath the surface. I've been pressing it down, determined to have the energy to do it all with a smile. But I realize that, though I've been working hard to prove I have no limits, I've also grown to resent the ways my limits are so often disregarded. So, when I feel terrible and people still need to eat, I become a ticking time bomb. I begin to understand those women who just get in the car and start driving.

One day, my husband and I were hanging out with my brother and his wife, and I confessed I sometimes pine for a medical emergency. The men looked alarmed. "Nothing major," I said, "just, like, an appendix. Something that requires a hospital stay so I can sleep for a few days." "Well *that's* not okay," my brother said, looking at his wife and assuming she'd be nodding along. Instead, she sheepishly replied, "I have that fantasy too."

I think we can all agree that something is wrong when we're hoping for organ removal just to have an excuse not to be needed for a little while.

EVERYONE SEEMS TO BELIEVE— OURSELVES INCLUDED—THAT WOMEN HAVE ENDLESS CAPACITY AND CAN DO AND BE ALL WITHOUT CONSEQUENCE.

We need to talk about what it means to be limited, to have a finite amount of time, energy, and attention to give away in whatever roles we fill. But it's complicated, especially for women, because everyone seems to believe—ourselves included—that women have endless capacity and can do and be all without consequence. I'm sorry to tell you this, and hesitant to believe it myself, but it's a lie! And no matter if we feel free or resentful, perfectly placed or pulled in a million directions, we probably also feel really, really tired. We need to embrace the dignity of being human, and I hope we'll find it's actually the pathway to connection and rest.

How Does She Do It All?

It's not difficult to find the roots of our struggle against limits. We saw in chapter 4 how our default mode under the covenant of works makes us want to hustle to prove our value. But even if we know we're not working to merit righteousness before God, we often don't notice the ways our values are inadvertently shaped by the world around us. The idols of achievement and self-sufficiency come for us all, especially in the West. Our culture prizes expressive individualism, and personal fulfillment, not communal well-being, is seen as the ultimate goal.

A SHIFT IN FOCUS

In some ways, this is an inherited struggle. As the Industrial Revolution moved work out of the home, it forged separate spheres for men and women, sending men out and keeping women in. Where men and women had labored side by side in families and communities, sharing the physical and emotional burden of eking out a living, raising children, and otherwise building a life, now men worked long hours in factories and offices while women kept kids and home. Homemaking was aided by the help of new appliances that made what was once backbreaking work—requiring multiple hands and hours—both easy and tedious. Many women felt robbed of their sense of purpose and ability to contribute in meaningful ways.

Frustrated by their new exclusion and growing isolation, a generation of homemakers resonated with what Betty Friedan labeled "the problem that has no name" in her 1963 book, *The Feminine Mystique*.[1] At the time, Friedan provided language for

LIMITED

those who couldn't put their fingers on the source of their boredom and resentment, depression and aimlessness. This gave rise to the second wave of feminism. While the first wave of feminism focused primarily on women's right to vote and own property, the second wave fought against the social and cultural limitations placed on women.

BALANCING DEMANDS

The second wave of feminism did achieve some important results, drawing attention to the father's important role in child-rearing, for example, and raising the issue of domestic violence, calling for abusive husbands and fathers to be held accountable. Further, Friedan and others' advocacy asked good questions about the unjust and unnecessary limitations placed upon women. But our attempts at women's liberation have sought to set us free from our limits, only to create a problem with new names. Today, we denigrate (or exaggerate) domestic responsibilities, engage in the "Mommy Wars" (between stay-at-home mothers and those who work outside the home), fight against the gender pay gap, question what women can do, and argue about what we can't. Opportunities beckon us, telling us we can do, have, and be it all, or challenging us to choose wisely and give up the rest—our families, our health, our sanity. And many women are finding their resulting realities unmanageable.

EVEN A UTOPIAN SOCIETY CAN'T CHANGE THE HOURS IN A DAY OR EMPOWER A PERSON TO BE IN SEVERAL PLACES AT ONCE.

Consider what we're dealing with: Journalist Brigid Schulte tells us that the American workplace has "an expectation of work without end" and "that workplaces expect all-out dedication of body, mind, and soul.... There is only one way to work to succeed or to survive," she adds: "all the time."[2] And, lest we think it's only the workplace that requires this kind of all-in commitment, we're living in the age of the "expert mom." "Maternal instinct isn't just about mom love anymore," journalist Jessica Valenti writes. "It's a built-in expectation that truly loving and committed mothers are the absolute authority on everything having to do with their children—down to the very last dirty diaper."[3]

To be even partly true that we can achieve the balance we crave between home and work, to name just two roles many women inhabit, it would require a laundry list of changes within institutions and our own lives. And yet even a utopian society can't change the hours in a day or empower a person to be in several places at once.

It's not only women who face these endless demands, but we tend to think about men's and women's time and capacities differently. "There is a perception that men's time is finite, yet a woman's time is infinite."[4] This is in part due to the kinds of tasks that tend to fall to women, like caregiving and home-keeping, which are often undervalued and unnoticed yet still take time and mental energy. "An hour at the pediatrician's office holding a child's hand is just as valuable as an hour in the boardroom," Eve Rodsky says.[5] And I think the bigger point is that they both take an hour, and someone still has to get dinner on the table.

KEEP SMILING

Even as we wrestle with the pressures put on women, we pass down advice that perpetuates them. When I was still a relatively new wife, losing my mind at home with babies underfoot, well-meaning women advised me not to wake my husband to

LIMITED

help with the baby in the night; to be sure to tidy up and put on makeup before he comes home from work; to throw some onion and garlic in butter on the stove even if I don't have a dinner plan—"the promise of things to come"; and to always be ready for intimacy. While I don't doubt this kind of advice could be nuanced and helpful for particular seasons or circumstances, I internalized a message of self-sufficiency. *Don't show signs of struggle. Don't let your husband know you need him. Keep lipstick on and a smile on your face.*

We do this to single women too. I've heard friends lament their inability to be honest when they feel overwhelmed or exhausted because of the response they often receive: "You don't even know what busy is." They're expected to have endless time, to be the ones with the most to give, and especially, not to have needs of their own.

Where do we start in dismantling these harmful narratives and the unsustainable lives that result? Our culture offers one approach, peddling the lie that the unencumbered life is more free. It tells us to cast off what burdens us, namely, people. More and more people are delaying marriage, forgoing children, and choosing a life free from obligations to others. This is how second-wave feminism became so enmeshed with the sexual revolution. By advocating for birth control and abortion rights, Friedan and others fought to address the biggest hindrance to a woman's upward mobility—children.[6]

BURNED-OUT AND LONELY

But how is that working for us? Having grown up on the expectation of ever-optimizing and working-all-the-time, millennials have been labeled "The Burnout Generation."[7] One Gallup study showed that "about seven in 10 millennials are experiencing some level of burnout on the job," concluding that "today's typical workplace is chronically grueling, especially for the millennial generation."[8] "Millennial burnout often works differently among women," journalist Anne Helen Petersen writes, pointing to "the second shift" and "the mental load," borne especially by married women with children who "[take] on a role akin to 'household management project leader.'"[9]

This call to be unencumbered and our subsequent obsession with work has left us achingly lonely. The US Department of Health and Human Services reports on the fundamental human need for social connection and the corresponding risks to our health and longevity when we live in isolation.[10] "Approximately half of U.S. adults report experiencing loneliness, with some of the highest rates among young adults," the report states, and studies found that "loneliness and social isolation increase the risk for premature death by 26% and 29% respectively," causing this epidemic of loneliness to be labeled a "critical public health concern."[11] Surely there are a number of factors influencing our growing isolation, but we shouldn't be surprised to find our attempts to defy limitations in pursuit of achievement and self-sufficiency have left us alone at the top, our relationships sacrificed on the altar of individual fulfillment.

We are constantly needed, but we're not supposed to need anyone. We're resentful and overburdened, burnt-out and isolated. We have constructed a façade where no one is allowed to be honest about how desperate we actually are. But we do ourselves and one another a disservice when we pretend to be superhuman. God has created us with a diversity of gifts and interests; He's entrusted us with different seasons and responsibilities. But He's also created us with limits.

LIMITED

Limits Are for Your Good

In chapter 4, we considered the way covenant theology helps reframe our work. Because Christ has achieved righteousness for us, we don't work to earn God's favor but rather to be His instrument of grace in the lives of our neighbors. This is the theological answer to our problem, leading us to the source of rest we long for and transforming our work from a burdensome toil to a source of purpose and joy.

It's not just what motivates our work that's a problem, though. It's also that we don't know when (or how) to stop.

In the opening chapters of Genesis, God shows He is the author of limits. Creation is not a free-for-all. Every created thing has a place and boundaries allow for flourishing.[12] We've seen that even the created order is meaningful, establishing authority structures for our good. God establishes a pattern of work followed by rest, not because He was tired, but because He knew we would be. He made us as humans, not gods. He gave us twenty-four hours in a day and bodies that require food, water, and sleep.

TRUTH BE TOLD, I'VE NEVER BEEN A BIG FAN OF THIS IDEA OF MATERNAL INSTINCT.

Nonetheless, our lives constantly tempt us to defy our humanity. We're pulled in a million directions, bearing the emotional weight and physical needs of lots of people, whether in our homes, churches, or workplaces (or all of the above). Many of us feel daily the depletion of our literal bodies as we pour out on behalf of others. We can face our humanity all we want, but the list of needs will keep piling up. This is not an invitation to live without limits, however. Rather, God has this way of patiently bringing us to the edge of our capacity so we can learn to "rely not on ourselves but on God who raises the dead" (2 Cor. 1:8–9).

147

Dependence on God is one of those biblical truths that sounds good but feels intangible. How do we know if we're relying on God? What does His help look like? The idea of maternal instinct provides a good example for the lesson we all need to learn here.

Truth be told, I've never been a big fan of this idea of maternal instinct. It implies some inherent mothering ability within all women, some sixth sense that emerges when you have children. This is largely unhelpful, shaming women who don't consider themselves natural nurturers on the one hand, and on the other, silencing mothers who can't find everything they need for the overwhelming work of motherhood within themselves. "You'll know exactly what to do," we tell each other as we welcome new babies into the world. At the time of this writing, however, I'm nearly eighteen years into this mothering thing, and I can tell you with utmost confidence that I still don't know exactly what to do.

Over the years, though, I've discovered it's not the idea of maternal instinct itself that's wrong, it's the way we've allowed our individualism and self-sufficiency to redefine its meaning.

I can remember one particularly rough night as a new single mom. My daughter and I sat in the bedroom we shared in my parents' house. Hadley screamed, I bounced. She screamed more, I nursed. She screamed, I cried and bounced some more. At one point, I laid my screaming baby down on my bed and crumbled to the floor. I didn't know what to do. I was exhausted and helpless and felt so alone.

We persevered that night, just the two of us. Still awake in the early morning, I brought out my baby (who, admittedly, I didn't particularly care for at that moment) as soon as I heard my mom get up. My mom extended her arms, and I dissolved into sobs. I felt so much shame—that I couldn't figure out what my baby needed, at the resentment burning in my heart, over my failures as a mother.

LIMITED

My mom held my daughter and hugged me and said what every woman needs to hear. Not, *You've got this. You'll know just what to do.* No, she said: "Why didn't you ask for help?"

With these words, my mom passed on to me the lesson she had lived by as a mother of five kids born within seven years, married to a fighter-pilot who was often gone. True maternal instinct is not relying on ourselves but knowing you must lean on others. I grew up surrounded by a village, and my children have too.

Depending on God doesn't mean we go back to bootstrapping in service to others while secretly hoping for a hospital stay. Instead, as we come face-to-face with our limits, we recognize that we can't do or be it all; we need a village. And God does us one better: He provides a church.

With All the Saints

It's clear from the beginning that God made us to need one another. It wasn't good that Adam was alone; he needed Eve (Gen. 2:18). This isn't just a Christian reality but a human one. Families and communities have existed since the beginning of time. To be isolated meant you were vulnerable and exposed, ill-equipped for the tasks of maintaining a life, not to mention lonely.

But this was especially true for God's people. When God called Abraham, it wasn't about Abraham as an individual but rather about forming a collective covenant people. God promised to make Abraham into a great nation that would become a blessing to others (Gen. 12:1–3). In the Old Testament, we see God's

GOD'S PROMISE ALWAYS POINTED FORWARD TO THE CHURCH, MADE UP OF PEOPLE FROM EVERY TRIBE, TONGUE, AND NATION.

faithfulness to His promise, establishing the nation of Israel and preserving a remnant even when their disobedience led them into exile. But this promise was never meant to end with the nation of Israel; it always pointed forward to the church, made up of people from every tribe, tongue, and nation.

There's just one problem. Following Jesus often means leaving behind "house or brothers or sisters or mother or father or children or lands" for His sake (Mark 10:29). Does this mean God's people are destined to live cut off from their communities in isolated dependence on God but not others? No, quite the opposite. Jesus says there is no one who's left everything to follow Him "who will not receive a hundredfold now in this time, houses and brothers and sisters and mothers and children and lands, with persecutions, and in the age to come eternal life" (v. 30). *Now in this time!* He's not pointing to an eternal reality but an earthly one. For all the ways Christians are sure to suffer as exiles living in a fallen world, loneliness need not be one of them.[13]

WE AND Y'ALL

To understand the implications of the shared life God has called us to, one of my favorite places to go is the book of Ephesians. Our communal identity is embedded in Paul's language—rather than using "I" and "you," he uses the collective "we" and "y'all."

God has blessed *us* with every spiritual blessing (Eph. 1:3).

Though *we* were dead in our trespasses, God made *us* alive *together* with Christ (Eph. 2:5).

He introduces us to three metaphors for the church, each illustrating how we belong to Christ and one another: The church is Christ's body and He is the head (Eph. 1:22–23); we are members of God's household (Eph. 2:19); and, with Christ as the

LIMITED

cornerstone, we are joined together into a structure, God's temple, "a dwelling place for God by the Spirit" (Eph. 2:20–22).

For many of us, the church is merely the collection of people we worship alongside on Sunday mornings, or even the broader cloud of witnesses across the world and throughout the ages. This is true in part, but it's more than an abstract reality that has no claim on our daily lives. Paul's pictures imply an interdependence that flies in the face of our Western ideals of individualism and self-sufficiency. We don't just exist alongside one another; we have a stake in each other's well-being, an investment in each other's spiritual growth, a claim to each other's resources. Paul prays that the Ephesian church "may have strength to comprehend . . . what is the breadth and length and height and depth, and to know the love of Christ that surpasses knowledge, that you may be filled with all the fullness of God" (Eph. 3:18–19). How will they understand the depths of God's love? By experiencing it "with all the saints" (Eph. 3:18). Dependent on Christ, we learn to depend on one another, and this teaches us about God's love for us. We become the tangible ears, mouth, hands, and feet of Jesus to our brothers and sisters.

HANDS AND FEET OF JESUS

This is something I know firsthand. Several years ago, my husband and I had reached the end of our rope. At the time, we were less than a handful of years into our marriage, and we had walked through two births and two miscarriages. Our three lively kiddos had been joined for the past year by an extra three-year-old through foster care. We lived in the country in a hundred-year-old farmhouse that couldn't handle the Minnesota winters (and really, neither could I). We were overwhelmed and decided it was time to close our foster care license, move into town, and embrace a simpler life.

So, obviously, we bought a house that needed complete updating. We moved in, tore out all the trim and flooring, picked paint colors, and lived in the basement while we slowly started our projects.

And then we found out my mother-in-law had stage 4 breast cancer. Unable to undergo any treatment, she entered hospice care, and we spent every moment we could with her and my husband's father and brothers. As sweet as those last months with her were, living in a torn-apart house with no capacity to make progress after an already-wearying season began to take its toll on us. We would try to squeeze projects into the crevices of our disappearing time, but we lived in a constant state of upheaval.

Thankfully, we belonged to a church and lived near our family, and God's grace showed up in ways we could see and taste and touch. Through shared tears and lingering hugs and hands ready to help. Through gentle words of rebuke and comfort and wisdom. Through homemade soup and crusty bread delivered at just the right time. Through His people.

While we banked priceless hours with my mother-in-law, our church family faithfully brought meals, chipped ice off of our driveway, painted our walls and, in what is still one of the sweetest acts of generosity I've been privileged to witness, rounded up a crew of people to come finish our floors so we could actually move into our bedroom and use our kitchen.

This is just a small glimpse into the many ways we have experienced God's grace through the generous love of church members over the years. Stubborn though I am, I have learned through one wearying season after another what it means to depend on God: It means honestly facing your limits. And it means being willing to need His people.

LIMITED

THE FOUNDATION OF HUMILITY

As magical as it might sound to live among a caring and involved church body, it's not without effort and sacrifice. After a few chapters spelling out our shared blessings as members of Christ and one another, Paul goes on to tell us how we're to live as God's people, and His commands center on how we're to relate to one another, to live faithfully side by side. He starts with what we need most if we're going to rightly live alongside "all the saints"—we need "all humility" (Eph. 4:2).

Humility is the foundation of life in Christ. Only people who recognize their need understand the good news of the gospel. This is why Paul walks the path he does through Ephesians 1–3: He shows us the depths of our need apart from Jesus as enemies of God and those alienated from one another (Eph. 2:3, 12). This awareness prepares us to marvel at God's abundant grace for sinners (Eph. 2:4–9). We have no grounds for boasting (Eph. 2:9) because we recognize that the ground is level leading to the cross. Being humbled before God teaches us to be humble before others.

"God opposes the proud but gives grace to the humble," the Bible tells us (1 Peter 5:5), and I think, at least in part, this means that pride cuts us off from the grace of God's provision through His people. In our pride, we cling to self-sufficiency, refusing to admit we can't do or be it all. But "with all humility," we accept the reality of our weaknesses and limitations. We learn to ask for and receive help, and as God's people show up, we find it's as if we're visited by Christ Himself.

Your Village Needs a Woman

Women play a crucial role in cultivating a life spent "with all humility" and "with all the saints." When I think back to all the help we received in that season, I recall several men who generously gave their time, muscles, and skills to care for us. But you know who was primarily responsible for making it all happen? The women. Dear friends intuited the needs, coordinated the details, showed up, and worked hard alongside the husbands, brothers, and friends they recruited to be there.

Many of us might resent the ways we see needs, the emotional weight we carry on behalf of our people, the logistics and details that so often fall to us to coordinate. And certainly humility requires us to ask for help even with these things that might feel natural, though no less overwhelming. But one fascinating study found that, in response to stress, instead of "fight-or-flight," women may respond instead with "tend-and-befriend."[14] "Tending involves nurturant activities designed to protect the self and offspring that promote safety and reduce distress; befriending is the creation and maintenance of social networks that may aid in this process," the researchers summarize.[15] These behaviors are rooted in our biology—our sex hormones impact how we respond to stress, and awareness of our vulnerability positions us to be more attuned to our need for others.[16]

> *Across the entire life cycle, females are more likely to mobilize social support, especially from other females, in times of stress. They seek it out more, they receive more support, and they are more satisfied with the support they receive. . . . Adult women maintain more same-sex close relationships than do men, they mobilize more social support in times of stress than do men, they rely less heavily than do men on their spouses for social support, they turn to female friends more often, they report more benefits from contact with their female friends and relatives . . . and they provide more frequent and more effective social support to others than*

LIMITED

do men. . . . Women are also more engaged in their social networks than are men.[17]

Deborah Tannen, who observes the differences in verbal behavior between men and women we considered in the previous chapter, points out that women are also generally more willing to ask questions. She writes, "Of all the observations I've made in lectures and books, the one that sparks the most enthusiastic flash of recognition is that men are less likely than women to stop and ask for directions when they are lost. I explain that men often resist asking for directions because they are aware that it puts them in a one-down position and because they value the independence that comes with finding their way by themselves."[18] In other words, a woman's openness to seeking help and asking questions positions her to cultivate relationships with those around her, benefiting not just herself and other women, but also the men and children in her community.

Though we all have different personalities, backgrounds, and opportunities, I love these testimonies from nature about how God designed His female image bearers to provide the relational glue for communal life. As the Lord builds His church and through it provides for His people, what if God equips spiritual moms and grandmas, wives, aunts, sisters, and daughters with insight into the community's needs, not so we can handle it all, but so we can leverage our unique strengths to help build the relational networks God will use to sustain us all?[19] What if we defied the narrative that we're meant to do life on our own and instead lead the way "with all humility," being the first to ask for help?

Lead with Need

Whenever I describe the rich community life I've been blessed to be a part of, I'm often met with stories from disappointed people who have been unable to forge these kinds of relational networks. I've certainly experienced seasons where I've felt isolated, unsure of who in my community to list on my kids' emergency contact forms. Leaving the church community that remodeled our house (and the proximity to my biological family) to move across the country and go to seminary is a grief that still lingers eight years later. It took time to build a new network, and just as it felt like we had found our people, we graduated and faced new fresh starts and the loneliness that comes with them.

Over the years, I've found that different seasons have made it easier or more difficult to form the family-like relationships where people show up for one another without needing to ask. My years at home with young children were particularly hard for me, and my desperation humbled me quickly. I asked for help frequently because I lived with constant awareness that I was out of my depth. This helped a community to form around us, poised to be the rescue boat that would carry us through my mother-in-law's illness.

In seminary, too, we lived in a community of people stretched to the point of breaking and left with no room for pretense. We all felt keenly our need for Jesus and our need for each other, and this knit us together quickly.

As my kids have gotten older, though, and we live in a more sprawling community where traffic and schedules make it difficult to do daily life alongside the members of our church, it's taken longer to form the kind of relationships I had with toddlers around. Only a few people know me well enough to know that the first thing I need when life falls apart is a home-cooked meal I didn't have to make. It feels more vulnerable to admit I need help.

I shared as much with some women in my church community after my husband suddenly collapsed on a family outing. He's fine; everything was fine. But it sure didn't feel like it at the time. I had a friend visiting from out of town, which made caring for my children alongside getting my husband to the ER manageable. But, I admitted, if she hadn't been there, I didn't know who I would call. I choked back tears, fearful I had overshared, unsure how this group would respond. But later that night, I received a message from a woman in my church: "If Jordan ever passes out again, call me right away."

IN EACH SEASON, I'VE HAD TO RELEARN HOW TO BE NEEDY, AND HOW TO EMBRACE THE VULNERABILITY OF SHARING MY NEEDS.

In each season, I've had to relearn how to be needy, and how to embrace the vulnerability of sharing my needs with people who might not rise to meet them. But in each season, I've also found that God is faithful to provide through His people. We need only show up in humility. I haven't always been met with the help I was looking for, or with any help at all. Sometimes my vulnerability has hung in the air, leaving only lingering awkwardness. Nonetheless, when we take the courageous step to go first "with all humility," to lead with our own needs, I have found more often than not it creates an environment of invitation—for others to admit the ways they fall short, and for us all to embrace the opportunity to be the body of Christ.

Know Your Limits

Even as we learn to see our limits clearly, to depend on God and one another, the fact is, the work will still be there. We might pour out until we're forced to stop, and then we'll have to take some decongestant and make everyone dinner. Knowing this is the case, I'd like to share some lessons I've learned from my village, wisdom shared with me by wise women who have patiently intervened as I've tried to run myself into the ground—or as I've ugly cried over another sick kid or impossible assignment or living room flood.

PRAYER IS ESSENTIAL

First, don't underestimate the power of prayer. Author Paul Miller tells us prayerlessness actually reveals our pride: "If you are not praying, then you are quietly confident that time, money, and talent are all you need in life. You'll always be a little too tired, a little too busy. But if, like Jesus, you realize you can't do life on your own, then no matter how busy, no matter how tired you are, you will find the time to pray."[20] Prayer can be our first act of humility, our white flag of surrender to our limits. Humbled before God, we cast our anxieties on him, remembering He cares for us (1 Peter 5:6–7). I often imagine myself in Jacob's place, wrestling with God. My prayers are me clinging to Him for life, crying out, "I'm not letting go until you bless me!" This picture of desperation keeps me rightly positioned before God, ready to recognize His help when He gives it, even if it's just strength to get through another impossible day.

WE MIGHT POUR OUT UNTIL WE'RE FORCED TO STOP, AND THEN WE'LL HAVE TO TAKE SOME DECONGESTANT AND MAKE EVERYONE DINNER.

I've been tempted at times to only value the tangible help God provides through His people, frustrated at how "not helpful" it is when someone just responds to a need with "I'll pray for you!" But when the apostle Paul was imprisoned for the gospel and facing the likelihood of death, he wrote, "Yes, and I will rejoice, for I know that through your prayers and the help of the Spirit of Jesus

Christ this will turn out for my deliverance" (Phil. 1:18–19). Paul was confident that the prayers of His brothers and sisters were exactly what the Lord could use to sustain and provide for Him. I've come to value the prayers of others as an incredible source of support and comfort in trying seasons. And, knowing how it strengthens me to know that someone is praying for me, I've tried to turn my concern for others into prayers as well.

SERVE IN FAITH

Second, serve in faith. Proverbs 11:25 says, "Whoever brings blessing will be enriched, and one who waters will himself be watered." This fills me with such hope. As I pour out to others, I do so trusting that God is pouring into me. As I strive to be a blessing to others, even stretching beyond what I think I have within me to offer, I do so believing that "it is more blessed to give than to receive" (Acts 20:35), and "whoever sows sparingly will also reap sparingly, and whoever sows bountifully will also reap bountifully" (2 Cor. 9:6).

Time and time again, I have given more than I thought I could handle, finding in the process that I'm actually the one being blessed. The Lord works in and through us in these seasons of depletion and desperation, and as we serve in faith, we find as He multiplies our strength, He can also multiply our joy.

EMBRACE THE LIMITS

And finally, freedom comes when we embrace the limits of our seasons. We ought to pray for God's help and trust He will provide grace sufficient for our callings. But we also ought to take care to surrender to the limits of our seasons, not clinging to past callings or borrowing from future ones. This has been one of the hardest things for me to learn, and one for which I've needed other people to help me see clearly.

We don't prefer to think in seasons. It's hard enough to figure out the rhyme or reason of our daily lives, much less imagine the future, where we might have more capacity or different opportunities. So, instead, we try to fit everything in right now.

But there's a seasonality to our lives, and we aren't in control of it. In Ecclesiastes 3, the Preacher writes a poem meant to assure those of us trying to make sense of life's absurdity that, despite how it may seem, "For everything there is a season, and a time for every matter under heaven" (v. 1),

a time to be born, and a time to die;
a time to plant, and a time to pluck up what is planted;
a time to kill, and a time to heal;
a time to break down, and a time to build up;
a time to weep, and a time to laugh;
a time to mourn, and a time to dance;
a time to cast away stones, and a time to gather stones together;
a time to embrace, and a time to refrain from embracing;
a time to seek, and a time to lose;
a time to keep, and a time to cast away;
a time to tear, and a time to sew;
a time to keep silence, and a time to speak;
a time to love, and a time to hate;
a time for war, and a time for peace. (Eccl. 3:2–8)

His point is to rightfully position us before the God who orchestrates beginning to end (Eccl. 3:11). God has called us to embrace the limitations of wherever and whenever we find ourselves, and not only that, to see that His ordering of time and boundaries is beautiful (Eccl. 3:11). Pastor Zack Eswine tells us to learn from the Preacher of Ecclesiastes, to "open [our] hands, pay attention

LIMITED

to what God is giving and what he is not, [and] receive with humility what he gives as enough."[21]

It takes courage to surrender to the limits of our seasons, but as we do, we're set free from the burden of resentment. We learn to see that God has appointed these boundary lines, and so we say with David, "The lines have fallen for me in pleasant places; indeed, I have a beautiful inheritance" (Ps. 16:6). This, I think, is the humble life of joy God intends for His creatures, one where we trade self-sufficiency for community, achievement for prayer, and the wearying work of daily life into sources of blessing.

8

Secondary

ON HAVING A PLACE

> "Roz, what are you meant to do?"
> "I don't believe I have a purpose."
> "Ha! I respectfully disagree," said Swooper. "Clearly you are meant to build."
> "I think Roz is meant to grow gardens."
> "Roz is definitely meant to care for Brightbill."
> "Perhaps I am simply meant to help others."
>
> PETER BROWN, *THE WILD ROBOT*

I always dreamed of living and working overseas. I haven't traveled extensively, but I've been to some far corners of the world. I went to Guatemala on my first international mission trip as a freshman in high school, and I loved everything about it—experiencing a new culture, trying out a new language, seeing vast needs and believing I could be well-placed to help meet them. The summer between my junior and senior year of high school, I spent two weeks with missionaries in Chad, followed by two weeks in Pyatigorsk, Russia, volunteering in an orphanage.

After that, I was hooked. I went to college and began pursuing a degree in International Studies. By the time I graduated, I thought the path was the Peace Corps, and then probably law school. I wanted to work for the United Nations, perhaps assisting asylum seekers or advocating for refugee populations. This, I thought, would be my calling.

Revisiting Dormant Dreams

But an unplanned pregnancy meant I never finished my Peace Corps application. Instead, I moved home and took the first job that offered health insurance.

Several years later, married and with a few children—during that season where I worked for my church but did my best to squeeze it into early mornings and naptimes so as to not actually impact my family—I was invited to spend a couple of weeks in Nepal teaching an Old Testament survey class to a group of women. I couldn't believe it. An opportunity to revisit a dead dream, to taste the life I might have chosen if I'd had the chance. My husband encouraged me to go, and my mom signed up to come hold things together at my house while I was away. So I waited with eager anticipation for my renewed passport, watching the days tick by until it was finally time to go.

But as the trip neared, a quiet panic settled in. I wasn't afraid of the travel, the time in-country, or the teaching. I was afraid of reawakening a dormant desire, of finding myself misplaced. Confident the experience would be incredible, I feared coming home. I worried the trip would add to the angst I already felt trying to embrace my primary role as homemaker and mother.

I was afraid I would love it.

SECONDARY

Vocation Is Not Zero-Sum

My existential crisis was, at its root, my wrestling with the notion—upheld in some spaces and considered antiquated in others—that women must be restricted to particular roles and places. Taking extended time away from my family felt like stepping out of my lane. That's because, though we saw in the previous chapter that we tend to think of women's capacities as unlimited, on the flip side, we also tend to think of women's vocations as zero-sum. If, as some suggest, her place is in the home, then any endeavor outside of it takes away from her primary calling. If she loves her job or her opportunities to serve the church, that means she doesn't love (or at least loves *less*) the people she's supposed to be caring for.

I'm not just talking about working moms. Though women's vocations are most often considered in relation to their marital and motherhood status, this is unnecessarily limiting. When we hold up domesticity as the ideal role for women, we put a crushing weight on those for whom this calling is either undesirable or out of reach.

WHAT IS THE PLACE FOR THE WOMEN? THIS IS REALLY WHAT WE'VE BEEN WANTING TO KNOW ALL ALONG.

What is the place for the women? This is really what we've been wanting to know all along. We've considered our value and identity, what the Bible teaches about God's female image bearers. And we've talked a lot about our functions—what we uniquely offer with our bodies, words, and relationships, what it means to believe there is a place for our vulnerability, our voices, our limitations. But *where* do we do these things? What spaces are we meant to occupy? What spheres are appropriate for us (and is this even a necessary question)?

We need to circle back to our discussion of vocation, to consider how our commission translates into everyday callings we're meant to live out with courage. We need to resume our consideration of limits, honestly facing the ways we have boxed one another in. And we need to evaluate our deeply held beliefs about women's roles, whether we see them as secondary, zero-sum, or the most important thing about us.

(Re)defining Calling

We often use the word "vocation" interchangeably with "occupation," reducing it to how it relates to our nine-to-five jobs, to what is labeled and official. Maybe that's understandable. We were made to work, and the average person will spend 90,000 hours—or one-third of her life—doing paid employment.[1] But this choice of language means we tend to think of our jobs as our primary callings, the most important thing about us. Everything else is secondary.

Further, since the Industrial Revolution separated work from the home, giving rise to the men-as-breadwinner, woman-as-homemaker ideal, men and women are often allocated to "separate spheres," in what is lauded as "the most 'efficient' kind of family unit."[2] This doesn't mean women don't have paid employment, however. The so-called idealized family of the 1950s is out of reach for many. More and more people are remaining single. In traditional families, the cost of living often requires two breadwinners, not to mention that some moms just want to have jobs (and may have careers with higher earning potential than their husbands).

SEPARATE SPHERES?

Nonetheless, our post-industrialized reality has caused us to generally assign the separate spheres of home and work on the

SECONDARY

basis of sex. Broadly speaking, this, paired with our assumption that paid work is the most important work, often results in the view that men's paid jobs are primary and women's are secondary, since a woman's primary calling is at home. Unless, of course, she's required to handle both spheres on her own; then we're not really sure what to do with her.

It's no wonder women are often fighting to do and be it all, as we saw in the previous chapter. We're tired of being kept out of the most important places; we want to do work that matters, and it seems like that requires a paycheck.

But rather than wading back into the gender wars, I'd like to take a step back and reconsider our callings. Which calling is truly primary? Which spheres ought we to occupy? I think answering the former will help us answer the latter.

IT'S NOT ABOUT WHO IS PAID, BUT WHO IS CALLING. WE'RE JOINED TO THE LORD OF LORDS.

The Bible uses the language of calling to refer to the way Christ draws us to Himself. "Those whom he predestined he also called," the apostle Paul writes, "and those whom he called he also justified, and those whom he justified he also glorified" (Rom. 8:30). This alone ought to reorient how we think about primary and secondary callings as believers. It's not about who is paid, but who is calling. We're joined to the Lord of lords and King of kings, and as such we "are called and chosen and faithful" (Rev. 17:14). We are "called to belong to Jesus Christ" and "called to be saints" (Rom. 1:6–7).

PRIMARY CALLING, PRIMARY SPHERE

Viewing our calling to be Christians as primary doesn't translate to a higher status for those serving in vocational ministry, though. In the time prior to the Protestant Reformation, the priests and monks suggested as much, arguing that vocation (which comes from the Latin word meaning "call") was reserved for those engaged in spiritual service.[3] Theology professor Linda Peacore explains that "Martin Luther opposed this view of a 'special calling' or 'vocation' to the monastic life. He believed the call of God comes to each in their daily tasks."[4] Luther argued "that all Christians have a vocation," or calling from God, "and that every type of work performed by Christians can be understood as such."[5] Peacore continues, "For Luther, to be a husband, wife, child, or servant means to be called by God to a particular kind of activity. It means to have a vocation."[6]

OUR CALLINGS STRETCH ACROSS SPHERES, OVERLAPPING AND CONFLICTING AT VARIOUS SEASONS OF OUR LIVES.

We are all called to something earthly—to relationships and responsibilities—but when we view our calling to be Christians as primary, it reminds us why we work in the first place. Remember how the covenant of grace reframes our work? Instead of a means to merely achieve personal fulfillment, our vocations are for the benefit of our neighbors. If everything we receive comes from God, then it's meant to be shared. We don't actually own any of it.[7]

We are first and foremost called to be Christians, and this ejects us from our efforts to rank ourselves, our spheres, and our work. It also requires that we adopt a broader view of vocation, creating space for multifaceted callings "unique to our situation and giftedness."[8] We are limited by the hours in the day, and by the needs of the hour, but our callings stretch across spheres, overlapping and conflicting at various seasons of our lives. To be Christians situates us to see our circumstances as God's intentional

SECONDARY

appointments, to receive our opportunities (or lack thereof) as gifts from His hand.

If our primary calling is to be Christians, then it follows that the primary sphere to which we're all called is the church. As those practiced at elevating paid work and domestic life, though, this can be a little jarring. We're used to seeing ourselves in relation to our nuclear families and our workplaces, perhaps even our local communities. But we are called to be saints, and this makes us members of the household of God.

I am first and foremost a daughter, but not of Mike and Tracie—of the God of the universe. I am first and foremost a sister, but not of Krista, Jordan, Alisa, and Taryn—of the men and women in my local congregation, of the cloud of witnesses who have gone before me. I am a bride, but not simply of my earthly husband, Jordan; I am a member of Christ's church, and Christ Himself is my bridegroom. I am a mother, an auntie, a cousin, a friend, but not only for those to whom I'm connected by blood and proximity, but for those to whom I'm connected by the gospel.

This might seem like an unnecessary specification, but I'd argue it's incredibly important when we talk about a woman's vocation, especially because of the ways we think of churches as a collection of nuclear families, emphasizing a mother's role within her own household. Our families are important callings, as we will consider further in a bit, but when Jesus is summoned by His mother and brothers, he responds, "'Who is my mother, and who are my brothers?' And stretching out his hand toward his disciples, he said, 'Here are my mother and my brothers! For whoever does the will of my Father in heaven is my brother and sister and mother'" (Matt. 12:48–50). The church is God's household. We looked at this in the last chapter, seeing the beautiful ways God has given us to each other, and how women may be uniquely poised to help cultivate and fortify the connections between us. Here, I want us to think for a minute about the implications for our callings.

A LEVEL PLAYING FIELD

If our first calling is to be Christians and our primary calling is to the church, the playing field is level. We all—male and female, married and single, parents or not, young and old—have a place in God's household, standing side by side before the cross. We are joined to a new family, united to one another through our union with Christ. This means we all have an essential role. There are no secondary players, even if some callings feature more prominently than others. This is Paul's point in 1 Corinthians 12, when he describes the church as Christ's body and believers as members of it:

> On the contrary, the parts of the body that seem to be weaker
> are indispensable, and on those parts of the body that we
> think less honorable we bestow the greater honor, and our
> unpresentable parts are treated with greater modesty, which
> our more presentable parts do not require. But God has so
> composed the body, giving greater honor to the part that
> lacked it, that there may be no division in the body, but that
> the members may have the same care for one another. If one
> member suffers, all suffer together; if one member is honored,
> all rejoice together. (1 Cor. 12:22–26)

Let's pause for a moment and consider how this elevates the single people in our midst, the church members who often view themselves as secondary, and who may be some of our loneliest and most isolated. First, those who are single reflect our eternal

SECONDARY

state (Matt. 22:30). Just as marriage offers a picture of the gospel for the church and the watching world (Eph. 5:22–33), so singleness offers a picture of the life we anticipate in glory, where our devotions are undivided (1 Cor. 7:32–34). Paul says that each of these states is a gift (1 Cor. 7:6). And let's not forget also that Jesus was single, and the life and ministry of singles reflects His. Second, viewing ourselves as members of one household reorients how we think about our responsibilities to one another. "Family life" moves into a larger scale.

I've had the privilege of seeing this play out in some really beautiful ways. When I first became a Christian as a single mom, I was quickly welcomed as family. This showed up in two ways: I started attending a small group, and while members of the church poured love and attention into my daughter, others opened the Scriptures with me, letting me ask a million questions. Over time, we felt like we belonged, like these were our people, and the deficiency I felt as a single mother faded into the background.

I was also invited into a particular nuclear family. Hadley and I would join family dinners and were welcomed into whatever evening festivities were in store. Here, we had the opportunity to observe the rhythms of family life, to both learn and benefit from their love for one another. Several times, the dad would take all the kids to a park and, as he acted like a dad to my daughter too, he filled a void in her life that I couldn't provide on my own. When I met my now-husband, he joined the family too, and this couple acted as my protective big brother and sister. They walked alongside us as we dated, provided premarital counseling, and played a huge role in our wedding. And they stayed by our side through miscarriages and births, marital trials, and church struggles (and were the ones responsible for facilitating our house remodel during my mother-in-law's illness).

I've also witnessed this more recently at church. When someone leaves their nuclear family to go sit alongside the mom with kids in the pew whose husband is deployed. When single women sit alongside a recent widow every Sunday, warming the seat where her husband sat not long ago. When people talk to my kids like they're simply aunts, uncles, and grandparents invested in the lives of their own nieces and nephews or grandchildren. In these ways and more, we engage in family life as God intended.

We saw how, in the covenant of grace, the commission to "be fruitful and multiply" takes on a spiritual dimension, to "go therefore and make disciples of all nations" (Matt. 28:19). This is our mission, carried out as a body, and it relates to our work and relationships both inside and outside the church. We draw in the lost and we care for one another. When we think of the importance of mothers, sisters, and aunties, we should be thinking not simply in terms of earthly households but the spiritual one of which we are a part. Our other callings flow from there and to there.

WE DRAW IN THE LOST AND WE CARE FOR ONE ANOTHER.

Your Place in the Church

We often think of women's place in the church in terms of confinement and restriction. Both men and women can be guilty of this. As women, we can focus on what we're being kept out of, what feels unfair, and what often *is* unjust. Men may worry about holding the line, fearing that a woman who gives announcements will soon be giving the sermon. This is to our shame, reflecting neither the heart of God nor the witness of Scripture. We've seen throughout this book how the Bible calls women to discipleship and agency. And we've seen the many ways women have contributed to the church throughout history, by stewarding their

SECONDARY

vulnerability and their voices, occupying official and unofficial roles, and faithfully showing up as biological and spiritual moms and grandmas, daughters and sisters.

A MISTAKEN FOCUS

Nonetheless, we continue to struggle with the areas labeled as off-limits. Why is that? I think there are a number of reasons, some more virtuous than others. In the best cases, we are concerned with faithfulness to Scripture. As denomination after denomination has liberalized over the past decades, forsaking the authority of Scripture and caving to the pressures of a society focused on freedom and autonomy, we're concerned to avoid following in their footsteps. We want to honor God with our obedience, to take seriously His commands.

Further, how to apply the passages that speak to a woman's role in the church are not all clear. So, in our zeal, we add on rules to make sure we don't transgress the boundaries. We are extra careful about the ways we allow women to use their gifts, especially in official capacities. In the worst cases, we've believed any number of lies—that everything ought to be equal, that God is holding out on us, that the role of pastor and the act of preaching are the most important callings and that our roles are less valuable.

Whatever the case, we become more focused on what women can't do, or perhaps on what they're permitted to do, rather than believing they are essential to the life and flourishing of the church.

NATURE AND STRUCTURE

To counter this, I think it's helpful to revisit the imagery Paul uses for the church in Ephesians.[9] In one particular passage, he seems to mix his metaphors:

A PLACE FOR YOU

So then you are no longer strangers and aliens, but you are fellow citizens with the saints and members of the household of God, built on the foundation of the apostles and prophets, Christ Jesus himself being the cornerstone, in whom the whole structure, being joined together, grows into a holy temple in the Lord. In him you also are being built together into a dwelling place for God by the Spirit. (Eph. 2:19–22)

Paul points to grounding, using the language of a building. But he also describes growth, like that which takes place in a garden. This highlights the dual nature of the church, its organic nature but also its institutional structure. As we think about the place for women to serve in the church, we tend to emphasize the latter, focusing on authority structures and offices. But Paul shows us the church is both. We belong to an institution built upon the apostles and the ongoing ministry of the officers of the church, which Paul calls gifts for God's people (Eph. 4:11). But we also exist and grow organically as a household. We are members of a family, each given gifts by the Spirit to build one another up (Eph. 4:15–16).

Recall the purpose of metaphors. As we ponder what we understand of the earthly reality, it fills out our understanding of the spiritual one. When I think about the church as God's household, I picture past gatherings among extended family. There is joy at being together, an overarching priority of connection and care. But there's also a lot of bustling. My mom, grandma, aunts— and now the next generation of my sisters and cousins too—pour into the kitchen carrying trays of food, having coordinated for weeks about who would bring what. Grandpa is probably tending to the fire, or maybe making everyone popcorn, while my aunts and uncles gather the kids and fill out the bracket for the foosball

SECONDARY

tournament. Someone is probably getting a baby settled for a nap, while another is taking the dogs to run around outside. People are cozied up on the couch, sharing life updates over mugs of coffee, while others are setting up a board game, turning on the football game, prepping the food line, running to the store for something we forgot.

Even if these examples feel superficial, I'm guessing you can picture the scene—individuals coming together, each with something to offer, every person finding their place and going about it faithfully, without giving much thought to the roles others are filling. (In fact, they are likely taking for granted that others are just doing what needs to be done.)

This is how we ought to live out our callings within the church.

One of our family values is "contribution." You're part of a family, we tell our kids. We want that to shape in them a communal identity, to learn that being part of a family has implicit obligations. In our family, everyone benefits from the generous love and service of another. But also, everyone contributes.

> **YOU DON'T NEED SOMEONE TO TELL YOU WHERE YOUR PLACE IS. YOU SIMPLY NEED TO BELIEVE THERE IS A PLACE FOR YOU. IT'S WHERE YOU ARE. THAT'S YOUR CALLING.**

I wonder how it might change our perspective on a woman's place if we viewed it as an indicative statement instead of a question. You don't need permission. You don't need someone to tell you where your place is. You simply need to believe there *is* a place for you. It's where you are. That's your calling. To this church, these people, this season. Where has God placed you in His household? What gifts has He given you? To whom has He given you? What opportunities has He provided for you to encourage or teach, to listen and pray for others, to bring a meal or provide childcare, to give generously?

We must remember the limits of our seasons, the way our focus ebbs and flows as God gives us varied responsibilities. But as we understand our primary calling as Christians and our placement in God's household, the church, it begins to alleviate the angst we feel about finding our place.

The Church as an Institution

We have seen Paul's use of metaphor in describing the organic nature of the church, the way it functions as a household, needing and valuing everyone's contribution.

Now, what about Paul's other metaphor, the church as an institution? Here is where Paul restricts the participation of women, and we're tempted to focus on how we can keep them out. At the risk of oversimplifying what is a highly contested topic, I want to join the ranks of scholars who argue that we've made this far more difficult than necessary.

Let's revisit 1 Timothy 2. Paul writes, "I do not permit a woman to teach or to exercise authority over a man; rather, she is to remain quiet" (1 Tim. 2:12). One of the reasons we focus on what women can't do is because we see Paul restricting women from two activities here: teaching men and having authority over men. If this is the case, then these items are placed on a spectrum, and we start drawing lines to determine what women can and cannot participate in within the life of the church. What is teaching exactly? What constitutes authority?

I think we've overcomplicated this. Paul goes on in 1 Timothy to be more clear about what he means by teaching and authority. In the context of 1 Timothy, Paul is addressing the church gathered for worship (2:1–15). He goes on to give qualifications

SECONDARY

for elders (3:1–7). Among those qualifications is the ability to teach (3:2), where Paul uses the same root word from 2:12. What he has restricted women from in chapter 2, he now commends in chapter 3, showing that it's not all men who are called to this activity, but rather certain qualified and appointed men. He further expounds on what kind of teaching he has in mind in this context: He commends the pastors and elders who labor in preaching and teaching (5:17) and charges Timothy to put "the words of the faith and of the good doctrine" before the brothers (4:6), to "command and teach these things" (4:11), and to "keep a close watch . . . on the teaching" (4:16).

Paul is not referring to any kind of teaching in any context. Letting Scripture interpret Scripture clarifies that. He lists teaching among the spiritual gifts given to members of Christ's body for our mutual benefit (Rom. 12:6–8), and in Colossians, he tells all Christians to be filled with God's Word so we can teach and admonish one another (3:16). Here, in 1 Timothy, he's referring to the specific teaching function tied to the office of pastor/elder: defining the church's doctrine passed down by the apostles and preaching the Word in the gathered worship.

Regarding authority, the word Paul uses for "exercise authority" in 1 Timothy 2:12 is not used anywhere else in Scripture, and some have argued that Paul is restricting women from a particular kind of abusive or domineering authority. I don't think their arguments are convincing, but you can see the note for some references if you'd like to dig deeper.[10]

Though he doesn't use the same linguistic tie-in to fill out the picture of what he means by exercising authority as he does with teaching, Paul expands the idea conceptually when he goes on to describe the expectations for elders. Elders are called to be wise household managers (3:4–5), showing their competency to care for God's church (3:6). Among these elders are those who "rule well" (5:17). They guard the church's doctrine, being watchful for false teaching and keeping an eye out for wolves (1 Tim. 1:3–11; 4:1–5). And when people stray from the faith and continue in unrepentant sin, Paul tells them to exercise their authority for the good of the whole church: "As for those who persist in sin, rebuke them in the presence of all, so that the rest may stand in fear" (5:20).

So, when Paul says women are not permitted to teach or have authority over men, he's referring to the teaching and ruling functions of the office of elder, entrusted to qualified and appointed men. Elders are to exercise the keys to the kingdom: "the preaching of the holy gospel and church discipline."[11] Women are restricted from holding this office of pastor/elder and exercising these functions of teaching—defining the church's doctrine and preaching in the gathered worship service, and ruling—guarding the church's doctrine and exercising church discipline.

FUNCTIONS AND OFFICE

Paul specifies the functions, not the office, in 1 Timothy 2. He doesn't just say, "I do not permit women to be elders." People get hung up on this. But if Paul had only specified the office, it would have been possible for these functions to be exercised apart from it.[12] In spelling out the functions, he gets at the spirit of his instruction. We don't have to nitpick what women can do. Instead, we understand that women should not be elders, and they shouldn't do what elders do. They shouldn't preach in the gathered assembly or preside over matters of church discipline.[13] Beyond that, I'm persuaded that women are permitted to do in the church anything a non-elder man is permitted to do.[14]

In my denomination, this line is clearly and helpfully drawn

SECONDARY

through ordination, though that doesn't preclude us from having inconsistent application. When we hyperfocus on Paul's teaching regarding men and women to the neglect of his teaching regarding elder qualifications and proper order within God's household, we give the impression that the main qualification for teaching and having authority in the church is being male, rather than being a qualified elder. This results in all kinds of malpractice and becomes a legitimate source of hurt and frustration for sisters in the church. The answer, however, is not to dismiss Paul's teaching outright; it's to rightly apply it in reserving the functions of elders for the qualified men who have been called and appointed by the church.

FOUNDATION OF HEADSHIP

All of Paul's teaching about the institutional leadership of Christ's church is rooted in what we've seen about the Bible's foundation for headship, modeled after Christ Himself. It's not about power but about protection. The purpose of their rule is the care of God's people. Elders are to "shepherd the flock of God that is among you, exercising oversight, not under compulsion, but willingly, as God would have you; not for shameful gain, but eagerly; not domineering over those in your charge, but being examples to the flock" (1 Peter 5:2–3). They do this as those who will give an account to God for how they've borne responsibility for His sheep (Heb. 13:17).

Why does God restrict the role of elder to qualified men? I have some theories rooted in what we've observed about the primary differences between men and women being embodied. We've seen that Paul's teaching is rooted in creation, and his language of the household points to the metaphors God gives us to understand Him. As my pastor stands before me in his male body, he represents Christ to me, my elder brother. As my elders care for my soul, I see in their tender provision a picture of God my Father. God is not male—we know that male and female are both created in His image—but He condescends to our humanity, giving us these metaphors to help us understand Him. When these earthly realities reflect heavenly ones, it nourishes and strengthens our faith.

That said, the Bible isn't explicit about why this role is entrusted only to males. So I'm content to let my theories be theories and instead echo Kathy Keller's conclusion: "At the end of the day, I still don't know. I could speculate, but speculation often leads to error. I will follow that ancient divine who said, 'Where God has shut his Holy Mouth I will not venture to open mine.'"[15]

An Institution That Serves the Body

I have been working to clarify Paul's restrictions on women in Christ's church, because I think we often fixate on what women can't do, either fighting to overcome that one restriction or letting that restriction needlessly stretch across other spheres. Though the church as an institution restricts women from the office of elder, that doesn't mean we have no place within the institution. For one thing, we stand beside all members of the institution, male and female, benefiting from the ministry of its leadership. As these brothers, appointed by God, minister to us through Word and sacrament, Christ Himself works through them, nourishing us with His grace.

DEACONS

Christ also works through the institution, appointing officers for the care of His body. Though we all engage in family life, meeting

SECONDARY

each other's needs, Scripture calls certain men and women to serve the church in an official capacity as deacons. "Deacons in the early church were tasked with supporting the work of pastors by caring for the 'outward' or 'physical' concerns of church life," Pastor Matt Smethurst writes.[16] He goes on to quote historian Charles Deweese's summary of the deacons' role:

> *They visited martyrs who were in prison, clothed and buried the dead, looked after the excommunicated with the hope of restoring them, provided the needs of widows and orphans, and visited the sick and those who were otherwise in distress. In a plague that struck Alexandria about AD 259, deacons were described by an eyewitness as those who "visited the sick fearlessly," "ministered to them continually," and "died with them most joyfully."[17]*

It's disputed whether or not God calls women to this office, and there is a variety of interpretation and practice across different denominations and traditions. I'm persuaded that Scripture commends women as deacons (or deaconesses), and that church history testifies to a long history of deaconesses serving the church in significant ways. But my own denomination does not allow women to serve in this office and, for the sake of unity, I submit to its teaching. I do appreciate the ways my church and denomination have sought to bolster the participation of women in ministry and leverage the gifts of their female members for the benefit of the church in both official and unofficial capacities.

OF ALL PAUL'S LETTERS, ROMANS CONTAINS THE MOST ROBUST LIST OF HIS MINISTRY PARTNERS. OVER HALF ARE WOMEN.

I mention deacons here as an example of one way women might contribute in an official capacity. But whether as deaconesses or missionaries, church staff, teachers, writers, or any number of other formal roles, women's gifts are crucial for the flourishing of the church, the discipleship and care of its members, and the proper functioning of the church as an institution. No one knew this more than the apostle Paul himself.

Of all Paul's letters, Romans contains the most robust list of names, highlighting his ministry partners. Over half are women. He knows their names and their ministries, and he has personally benefited from them.[18] Phoebe is a servant of the church (the word is deaconess!) and also a patron, likely known for her generosity and hospitality (16:1–2). We know Priscilla and her husband Aquila as wise teachers from Acts 18:26, and in Romans, Paul commends them as "fellow workers . . . who risked their necks for my life," to the benefit of "all the churches of the Gentiles" (16:3–4). And, maybe my favorite, he greets Rufus' mother, "who has been a mother to me as well" (16:13). (Though I also love the language he uses for Euodia and Synteche in Philippians, describing them as having "labored side by side with me in the gospel" [4:3].)

OPPORTUNITIES TO SERVE

Have you read Romans 16 lately? Revisiting it just now brought tears to my eyes because it fills me with longing. Oh, that our churches would be places where qualified men serve as faithful pastors and elders, viewing both men and women in their congregations as partners in the gospel! Paul's ministry to, among, and alongside women ought to be a model for the church today. Just as a man who senses a call to pastoral ministry seeks confirmation within his church community, training at seminary,

SECONDARY

and opportunities to be called to serve Christ's church in a formal way, women who sense a call to vocational ministry can and should explore the myriad options before them. Go to seminary if you can. Seek the counsel of your pastor and church community. Pursue opportunities through your local church or consider the good work of parachurch ministries.

Pastors play a crucial role in coming alongside the gifted, godly women in their congregations. Whether these women are called to motherhood, the mission field, something else, or all of the above, a pastor's respect, encouragement, and investment are invaluable. I can attest to this note, included in the PCA's report on women in ministry: How a pastor responds to a woman's gifts "can either nourish or break the heart of a woman who is trying to serve God."[19]

Stewarding Our Homes

Properly situated with the church at the center of our Christian callings, we don't need to diminish our home-centered vocations. Though it can be tempting to idolize family life, to view motherhood as the pinnacle of our feminine existence, we must resist these distortions of God's good gifts. Nonetheless, the marriage and family life we share with the common realm provide a crucial stabilizing institution in society. And we all, married and single, male or female, need a home base from which we do daily life.

Let's be clear: The home is not a distinctly feminine sphere, nor is it the only feasible calling for a woman. Author Jen Pollock Michel points out,

> *Just as women are called to the care of their families and homes in Titus 2, so too are the male elders in 1 Timothy: "The overseer is to be . . . faithful to his wife" and "manage his*

*own family well and see that his children obey him," for "if
anyone does not know how to manage his own family, how
can he take care of God's church?" (1 Tim. 3:2–5). In fact,
male elders have an additional domestic responsibility: the
practice of hospitality, which is today often perceived as a
feminine call.*[20]

That practice of hospitality to which we're all called (Rom.
12:13)—men and women, married and single—creates a unique
opportunity to become a window for the watching world to see
Jesus. We've seen the ways marriage and singleness can teach us
about Jesus, but this is a picture I think we overlook: the family table. We all have a place in reflecting the church's invitation
to belong.

"YOU BELONG HERE"

This is something my parents practiced very well.[21] They
endured several years of suffering as I wandered away from my
faith. My feelings toward God ranged from ambivalence to hostility as I questioned everything I'd been taught to accept as true.
But even as they prayed for me and spoke the truth to me, calling
me to repentance and faith, they also did something else: They
made sure I knew I could always come home.

"You belong here," they preached to me, over and over again.
Despite the shame I was accumulating for myself as I ran from
God, they made sure I knew I could not outrun God's love—and
I could not outrun theirs. This unconditional love and belonging was an instrument the Lord used to keep me anchored to my
family and, eventually, to bring me back into His church. It's the
instrument He used to knit me to His people as I sat around other
dinner tables, learning more about who He is and how He works.

Our homes could be an instrument of God's grace in the lives of our neighbors, church members, and of course, our own children. When we pull a seat up to our family's table and say, "You belong here," we teach people about the beautiful diversity of God's family. *You might be different from us. You might not feel like you "fit in." But you belong here, nonetheless. We love and accept you not because of what you do, but because you belong to us.*

My husband and I have come to call this the "family gospel." The family gospel doesn't save anyone, but it has the potential to point people to two things: God's unconditional love for them in Christ, and the home that's always available to them in Christ's church. This is such a beautiful way to steward our place in our homes: As believers, we have a unique opportunity to demonstrate how the welcome we've received in Christ compels us to welcome others. As women, our skills as relational "weavers" equips us to start piecing together the "frayed social fabric" of our age.[22] And it starts by viewing our homes as an important sphere entrusted to us by God. For our children and our neighbors and all who long for a place at the table, we pull up a chair and say, "You belong here."

When There Isn't a Place for You

As wonderful as it is to recognize that God has a spacious place and glorious purpose for His daughters in every sphere, our lived realities often don't align. Our churches may restrict women from serving in official capacities or diminish the value of their contribution overall. They may say they value women but struggle to demonstrate it in practice.

It's also possible our convictions will shift over time, and we will gradually find that our differences make it difficult to persist in a particular community. We need wisdom to know how to navigate these circumstances, to discern whether God is calling us to persevere in faith and remain in our local church, or to leave in faith for a better fit where we can serve.

Paul's teaching in 1 Corinthians 7 is helpful here. He reminds us that God has placed us where we are: "Only let each person lead the life that the Lord has assigned to him, and to which God has called him" (1 Cor. 7:17). But he also says we're "not enslaved" (1 Cor. 7:15).[23] His guiding principle, then, is this: "God has called you to peace" (1 Cor. 7:15). Elsewhere he writes, "If possible, so far as it depends on you, live peaceably with all" (Rom. 12:18).

WE MUST BE CAREFUL NOT TO STIR UP DIVISION IN CHRIST'S CHURCH.

We all know families can get messy and can become dysfunctional. Abusive leadership is real; misapplication of God's Word is real; injustice is real. *And* we are sinful. We can be selfish and, frankly, wrong. We can be fixated on the specks in others' eyes while we ignore the plank protruding from our own (Matt. 7:3–5).

We must do the work to recognize and repent of our own sin, to graciously and patiently pursue helpful dialogue and healthy change. We must humbly and honestly confront sin and use the means God provides to address persistent unrepentance (Matt. 18:15–20). We must be careful not to stir up division in Christ's church. And we must seek the Lord and trust Him to provide wisdom and grace as we take each step.

Every circumstance is unique, and I can't advise you on the right course of action in your particular one. But I will say this: If you're not in an abusive or dangerous situation, and if your church faithfully preaches the gospel, I hope you will only leave through tears. Pray for your church and its leadership; invest deeply in your community; explain your concerns to the pastors and elders

SECONDARY

striving to speak the truth in love (Eph. 4:15). Persevere as long as you can, trusting that where opportunities don't exist, ultimately it is God withholding them. Seek to be faithful where He's placed you, using your gifts to serve wherever and however you can. And if, in the end, you must go, let it be in grief, not anger.

Called to Be Willing

Nepal was great. It was hard too. My older body didn't handle the travel with as much grace as my teenage self, and I missed my husband, children, and church family more than I thought possible. But I was also glad I went, not just for the joy of seeing women dig into the Scriptures, though that was incredible. I was glad I faced my fears of wanting more than my life.

I stared into the temptation to believe God's place for me was somewhere other than where He had me, and I found instead that He had been quietly at work in my heart, turning me into someone with new dreams, placing me among people who needed my gifts, and opening doors at the right time for me to step into new opportunities. He taught me—and is still teaching me—to trust that vocation is multifaceted, and that He provides enough grace for whatever He calls us to (Eph. 2:10; James 4:6).

I think I've said it in a number of ways already: There's a place for you. What that looks like is going to differ for all of us, married or single, with kids underfoot or launched, at different points in our lives and careers, in different geographical locations, and facing different economic, physical, and emotional realities. The point I've been trying to reiterate throughout every chapter is that God's place for His daughters is spacious and it's beautiful; we need only to receive it.

The wise woman of Proverbs 31 "works with willing hands" (v. 13), and I think this is the call for all of God's daughters: not to demand our place, but to step into it, to steward our circumstances in faithfulness to God and in service to our neighbors. As we find our place hidden in Christ, He transforms us into women who do our work willingly and joyfully, as if we're working for Him (Col. 3:1, 23), because, of course, we are.

Closing Thoughts
A LETTER FOR MY DAUGHTERS

*"You think your temper is the worst in the world; but mine used to be just like it."
"Yours, mother? Why, you are never angry!" and, for the moment, Jo
forgot remorse in surprise. "I've been trying to cure it for forty years, and
have only succeeded in controlling it. I am angry nearly every day of my life,
Jo; but I have learned not to show it; and I still hope to learn not to feel it,
though it may take me another forty years to do so."[1]*
—LOUISA MAY ALCOTT, *LITTLE WOMEN*

When my oldest daughter was born, I opened a blank journal and wrote a dedication: "For the chapter in my life beginning with Hadley." I knew having a daughter would change the trajectory of my whole life. It already had. But I couldn't have fathomed all the ways.

I've pondered that scribbled epigraph as I've written these chapters, thinking of this book as a kind of letter to my daughters. Above all others, I want to help them form conviction. I want them to launch from our home in all their vulnerability and glory, ready to face the world with courage. And despite my best efforts to cram everything I can into their developing brains, I know all too well that some lessons can't be learned until we're up close, feeling the pain and confusion of life in a fallen world.

I have the neatest little women growing up under my roof.[2] Light and fire, Hadley and Adrienne teach me more about who I want to be. They are strong-willed and smart, kind and generous; they are fearless in ways I couldn't imagine being when I was their age. And my admiration for them only fills me with greater zeal. Like Marmee, who comforts Jo by showing that she's not alone in her deepest struggles, I don't want to merely tell my daughters to persevere through hard things. I want to show them it can be done. I want to prepare them for those moments when the darkness threatens to quench the flames, to snuff out the light. I want to be there with a little kindling, ready to help relight the match.

What I want for my daughters is the same thing I want for you, and it's the same call I issued in the beginning: I want you to know your God, I want you to know your own mind, and I want you to believe there's a place in the church for you. So, like a mom running down her list of "one more things" before finally letting her daughter go off on her own, I offer a few closing thoughts as we go from here.

Know Your God and Your Own Mind

My first semester of seminary, I took a course called "Women in the Church, Home, and Society." My professor had us read from theologians on both ends of the spectrum and, if I'm honest, I really wanted to be persuaded away from the complementarian position. I read the papers. I revisited the passages. I let myself entertain different interpretations. At the end of the day, though, I just wasn't convinced.

My convictions still shifted in some ways. The process of studying for myself exposed my inconsistencies even while it validated

CLOSING THOUGHTS

some of my concerns. It invited me into a conversation with theologians and pastors, writers and teachers, and I held up their ideas beside mine, trying to look at them all through the lens of faithful biblical interpretation.

This book you hold in your hands is a pretty good summary of where I landed, and I've shared it with you because I'm convinced it's the true and beautiful story of a God who is good and who does what is good (Ps. 119:68). But *my* convictions are not ultimately the point. The point is the process of landing somewhere. It's being willing to be wrong and for our heroes to be wrong. It's having a posture of humility as we come before the Scriptures, believing they are God's very words and we must obey what they say. It's recognizing that we don't do biblical interpretation in a vacuum; we exist in community and in conversation with church history, and we must resist the urge to form our conclusions in isolation. But we also must be convinced in our own minds. Our obedience must flow from our own faith.

My challenge to you is this: Don't rely on someone else's understanding. If you're going to know your God, you're going to have to question Him, wrestle with Him, and trust He's strong enough to handle it. Dig into the hard passages of Scripture. Read widely. Invite wise counsel to come alongside you. Pray a lot. And trust that the Lord has good for you in the midst of the struggle. He is shaping you into a woman who knows Him, who loves Him, and whose mind is being shaped by the mind of Christ.

One more thing: Don't spend your life down the rabbit hole trying to figure out the place for women. I can attest to how easy it is to become so fixated on hard topics that we neglect to take a step back and see the broader sweep of what God is doing in His Scriptures, throughout history, and in our hearts.

It's good and right to work through hard truths, but what a shame if we lose sight of the main thing along the way. Christ Jesus came into the world to save sinners, and we stand side by side as those desperately in need of His cleansing power. Returning to the gospel again and again will be the very sustenance we need to persevere through the sticky spots. Studying the biblical text, learning about other doctrines, hearing stories of God's faithfulness in His church—these will fill out our convictions, persuading us not only of God's heart toward women but also of His mercy, justice, and power in all things.

Lay Down Your Selfishness

I spent a lot of my life trying to figure out how to take up less space, literally and figuratively. Prone to measure myself against others, I feared being too much or not enough. As I got older, this became even more complex. I quickly internalized that the way to a man's heart was to shrink my body and hide my brain. At times, I would rebel against this notion, determined I would not be the one to become smaller—he would have to. I unleashed all my passion and fury, feigning indifference about how I was being perceived.

Doesn't this picture the two extreme caricatures of women in the church, home, and society? On the one side, you have the silenced housewife who has shrunk herself so small as to be invisible, determined not to take up the space meant for her husband. On the other, you have the abrasive feminist who insists on being the loudest in the room, crowding out the men.

It kills me that both of these pictures have us thinking once again in zero-sum terms, believing there's not enough space.

I've become convinced that God has a spacious place for both men and women to flourish. He has given each of us interests and

CLOSING THOUGHTS

talents, experiences and perspectives, personalities and seasons, all that we would delight in His good gifts and use them to serve others. Certainly, He calls us to lay down our interests for others' sake (Phil. 2:4). But we don't lay down our dignity, our voices, or our contributions; we lay down our selfishness. We reorient ourselves. Instead of staring down our brothers and sisters, determined to measure ourselves against them, we turn so that we're standing before God. There—before His face—we find we are both small and great. United to Christ and joined to His body, we are humbled and bowed low, *and* we are raised and exalted.

If we're going to live faithfully as Christian women, we need to see ourselves rightly, *coram Deo*. This certainly means we will stop inflating ourselves as we recognize our place of desperate need before the God of the universe. But it also means we will stop shrinking ourselves. We will find there is enough room before Christ's cross for every repentant sinner. There is enough room in Christ's church for every gift and calling. And, as we look around at a hungry world in need of the nourishing truth of the gospel, we'll find there is also more than enough work to be done.

Persevere with Hope

"You have need of endurance," the writer to the Hebrews says (10:36), and this statement of bare fact makes me smile. Have truer words been spoken? And yet this, too, is the "one more thing" I want to say to you.

This is a hard life, and that's a gross understatement. We limp along on this fallen earth, bloodied and bruised, filled with longing. We are drowning in disappointment. And yet, the writer goes on: "But we are not of those who shrink back and are destroyed, but of those who have faith and preserve their souls" (Heb. 10:39).

I've often grown weary in my advocacy for women in the church. I have faced accusations and misunderstandings. I've bumped into selfishness and anger—my own, mostly, but also that of others. I have felt crazy, and I've wanted to throw in the towel. Maybe, someday, I will. On this fight anyway. Because, though I long to see women flourish as members of Christ's body, though I long for our churches to benefit from their perspectives, voices, and gifts, and though I long for my own daughters to avoid the pain of feeling overlooked and undervalued among God's people, my hope ultimately stretches toward something far greater.

I believe with my whole heart that there's a place for women in the church. But I also face no illusions: I will spend my life in imperfect churches among sinful people—myself chief among them. Our hope must not be in achieving some perfect application of our convictions or some ideal opportunity to use our gifts or share our perspectives. Our hope must be in Jesus.

Even if we're never able to serve in the ways we feel called, even if we feel misunderstood and invisible, even if we never quite feel like we've found our place, at the end of the day, we long for Jesus and we look to heaven. There's a place waiting for us there, where we'll stand beside our brothers, co-heirs to the grace of life (Gal. 3:28–29; 1 Peter 3:7).

For now, let's keep working to build communities where daughters are welcomed alongside sons, where everyone invited into Christ's family finds they have a seat at the table. Let's keep calling our daughters and all God's children to conviction and courage.

But, by God's grace, let's also lift our eyes beyond these temporal goals and point ahead to an eternal glory that awaits. In the end, we'll recall those pages of Genesis before the shadow falls, where a beautiful bride is adorned for her husband. Only now we'll find ourselves joined to her, glorious and radiant, ready to

CLOSING THOUGHTS

step once and for all into the spacious place prepared for us. And there, we'll finally see our Groom face-to-face.

Acknowledgments

If this book has been remotely helpful to you, it's because God has blessed me with an abundance of wise counselors, fierce supporters, and companions in this calling.

My sister Taryn has pored over these words as much as I have, sacrificing countless hours to sharpen my arguments, clarify my sentences, and tell me when I'd crossed the line into cheese, sap, or nonsense. Where you found beauty, clarity, or helpfulness, you have her to thank (along with my incredible Moody editors, Catherine Parks and Pam Pugh).

Taryn is more than just a partner in my writing process, though. She is the sister alongside whom I've worked out these ideas over the past fifteen years, ever since that first summer I returned to my faith and we drove around North Dakota taking photos, listening to sermons, and talking with Bibles open in our laps. She has preached the gospel to me more times than I can count, picking me up off the ground, dusting me off, and pointing me back in the right direction. Taryn, you are a woman of valor, the embodiment of conviction and courage, and I wouldn't have been able to write this book—or, let's be honest, do much of anything—without your boundless wisdom and encouragement. Thank you.

One of my favorite parts of writing this book was getting to recall the Lord's work in my life through His people. Brett Moser faithfully preached the gospel to me all those years ago, and then

A PLACE FOR YOU

he humbly invited me to develop a philosophy of women's discipleship with him. He was the first of many pastors, elders, professors, and bosses who have wisely shepherded me, challenging me to use the gifts God has given me for the good of His church. Charlie Hogstad, Stephen Donovan, Adriel Sanchez, Dennis Johnson, Josh Van Ee, Mike Horton, David VanDrunen, Joel Kim, Chuck Tedrick, Eric Landry, Mark Green, Collin Hansen, Ivan Mesa—thank you for your patience, mentorship, and efforts to instill confidence in me.

Dan and Michelle, your generosity in welcoming Hadley and me at your table and teaching me what it means to follow Jesus laid the foundation upon which God has grown my faith and love for His church. Your care for our family through so many seasons has become my paradigm for what it means that we belong to each other. Tim and Casey, Britta and Steven, you also showed me Christ's love in tangible ways across so many seasons, drawing me in even when I felt undeserving and broken. And Roxie, Jen, Kim, Hannah, and our Moorhead community group, thank you for walking alongside us. I thank my God in every remembrance of you. I hope you each saw your fingerprints on these pages.

It's easy for me to write about how to be a woman of conviction and courage because I'm surrounded by so many of them, especially among the women of North Park Pres. Your thoughtful questions, wise contributions, prayers, and texts have carried me through this season. Thank you to Aimee, Steph, Linette, Kathleen, Eydie, and Arden for taking the time to read this manuscript and share your thoughts.

My seminary classmates listened to me talk endlessly about women in the church, and yet they continued to engage, some of them even providing feedback on an early draft of this manuscript. Nate and Katie, Caley and Sabrina, Christian and Jolene, and

ACKNOWLEDGMENTS

John and Theresa, thank you for your friendship and sharpening.

My colleagues at Sola Media encouraged me to pursue writing this book, and my colleagues at The Gospel Coalition cheered me across the finish line. And so many writers-turned-friends have provided camaraderie and counsel through this process. I'm so grateful. Thanks especially to Justin Holcomb and Trillia Newbell for being willing to advocate for this proposal, and for Jen Wilkin and Jen Oshman for reading my words and instilling courage for the journey.

I have the most amazing parents and siblings who have faithfully preached the family gospel my whole life, reminding me over and over that I have a place to belong. The metaphors God uses to teach me about Himself and His family are so meaningful because of how rich those realities are in my life. Thank you for your consistent love, prayers, and pep talks.

And then there's the real hero. My dearest Jordan, I have the hardest time knowing how to thank you because I know this book cost you the most. And yet you have borne that cost joyfully, fighting for this book with me. You have endured countless hours and an abundance of words as I've processed these ideas over and over again (for years!). You have held me through the tears of being misunderstood, silenced, and humbled. You have accompanied me through more than one uncomfortable confrontation; you have advocated for me; you have sharpened me; you have believed in me. You have done so many dishes. You have taught me about the beauty of Christ's headship and the kindness of His patient, sacrificial love. You are one of His greatest gifts to me. I love you.

Hey kids, your mom wrote a book! I couldn't have done it without you. Thank you for your sacrifice and support, for asking about word counts and encouraging me when I didn't feel like

I could keep going. Thank you for persevering through another season of too much In-and-Out and letting me miss out on some fun. And thanks for celebrating with me at every step along the way. It's one of my greatest joys to get to be your mom.

Finally, for all the prayers, help, and support that have made this book come to fruition, at the end of the day, if you found it helpful, it's because God delights in working through weak and flawed instruments to accomplish His purposes. I am the chief of sinners, but my God abounds in mercy. I pray you've found in these pages a testimony of Christ's perfect patience toward all who believe in Him.

To the King of the ages, immortal, invisible, the only God, be honor and glory forever and ever.

(1 Timothy 1:17)

Notes

Chapter 1: Beckoned

1. Because I hold to complementarian convictions (which I'll expound on throughout later chapters), I don't believe reserving the office of elder for qualified men is oppressive to women. I also believe that male eldership may result in some spaces where women's voices are not physically present. If we don't have formed convictions here, we might mislabel the good practice of ordained male officers as treating women as second-class citizens. However, often these male-led spaces neglect to value the perspective and contribution of the women in their midst, and this is where many experiences of church hurt begin. Further, there is a grievous number of cases where male leaders have exploited their authority, resulting in abusive and oppressive dynamics for men, women, and children in the congregation.
2. R. C. Sproul, "What Does 'Coram Deo' Mean?," Ligonier Ministries, November 12, 2017, https://learn.ligonier.org/articles/what-does-coram-deo-mean.
3. I love this language from Abigail Favale, *The Genesis of Gender : A Christian Theology* (Ignatius Press, 2022).

Chapter 2: Wanted

Epigraph: Lucy Maud Montgomery, *Anne of Green Gables,* 1908.
1. L. M. Montgomery, *Anne of Green Gables* (Sterling Publishing Co., 2016), 29.
2. Montgomery, *Anne of Green Gables*, 55.
3. Frank Newport, "Slight Preference for Having Boy Children Persists in U.S.," Gallup, July 5, 2018, https://news.gallup.com/poll/236513/slight-preference-having-boy-children-persists.aspx.

A PLACE FOR YOU

4. Elizaveta Sivak and Ivan Smirnov, "Parents Mention Sons More Often than Daughters on Social Media," *Proceedings of the National Academy of Sciences* 116, no. 6 (2019): 2039–41, https://doi.org/10.1073/pnas.1804996116.

5. "Female Infanticide in India and China," Gendercide, http://www.gendercide.org/case_infanticide.html. This has left a gender gap of 35 million in China and 25 million in India. See Rebecca McLaughlin, *The Secular Creed: Engaging Five Contemporary Claims* (The Gospel Coalition, 2021), 76.

6. Rodney Stark, *The Rise of Christianity: A Sociologist Reconsiders History* (Princeton University Press, 1996), 95.

7. It's important to note that these stories are descriptive, not prescriptive. They describe life in a fallen world and serve as a condemning record of God's people, pointing to their desperate need for a Savior.

8. From the 2023 film *Barbie*. See Yvonne Villarreal, "Read the Stirring Monologue About Womanhood America Ferrera Delivers in 'Barbie'," *Los Angeles Times*, July 23, 2023, https://www.latimes.com/entertainment-arts/movies/story/2023-07-23/barbie-america-ferrera-monologue.

9. This is a fan theory shared with us by a friend. I'm not sure its original source, but we think it's a lovely possibility, even if it doesn't reflect Lin Manuel-Miranda's intent.

10. Abigail Favale, *The Genesis of Gender: A Christian Theory* (Ignatius Press, 2022), 225.

11. David VanDrunen, *Divine Covenants and Moral Order: A Biblical Theology of Natural Law* (Eerdmans, 2014), 40.

12. Sally Lloyd-Jones, "Teaching Children the Bible," Key Life, June 11, 2014, https://www.keylife.org/articles/sally-lloyd-jones-teaching-children-the-bible/.

13. Michelle Lee-Barnewall, *Neither Complementarian nor Egalitarian: A Kingdom Corrective to the Evangelical Gender Debate* (Baker Academic, 2016), 126–45. Though we land in somewhat different places, Lee-Barnewall's literary approach to Genesis 1–3 has been deeply formative for my own reframing of these chapters in Genesis.

14. I'm grateful for Kathy Keller's book *Jesus, Justice, and Gender Roles* (Zondervan, 2012), which first introduced me to this distinction between justice and theology. Our experiences tend to lead us to think through these questions through the lens of justice, but we must start with theology.

Notes

15. Colin Gunton, *The Triune Creator: A Historical and Systematic Study* (Edinburg University Press, 1998), 9–10. Quoted in Don C. Collett, *Figural Reading and the Old Testament: Theology and Practice* (Baker Publishing Group, 2020), 120.
16. There's actually a lot of debate throughout church history and across traditions about what it means to be made in the image of God. I'm presenting here what I find to be the most compelling approaches, but Bavink's *Reformed Dogmatics* provides a helpful jumping-off point if you want to dig deeper into other views.
17. Herman Bavinck, *Reformed Dogmatics, Vol. 2: God and Creation* (Baker Publishing Group, 2004), 530.
18. Bavinck, *Reformed Dogmatics*, 557.
19. We'll look more at this vocational aspect in chapter 4.
20. Richard Phillips, "Man as the Image of God," The Gospel Coalition, https://www.thegospelcoalition.org/essay/man-as-the-image-of-god.
21. Though I've lost track of where, I first heard Jen Wilkin make this observation many years ago.
22. Henri Blocher, *In the Beginning: The Opening Chapters of Genesis* (InterVarsity Press, 1984), 100.
23. Matthew Henry, *Commentary on the Whole Bible*, https://www.biblegateway.com/resources/matthew-henry/Gen.2.21–Gen.2.25.
24. It's always difficult when we look to the creation account to establish norms because Adam and Eve represent both the first covenant community and the first marriage. It's important to note that God's statement here about Adam's aloneness is about more than marriage; it's about community. We are created to need one another, which we'll dig into further in chapters 7 and 8.
25. I need you to know that I did share bites of cookie dough, lest you think I'm a total monster.
26. Portions of this section have been adapted from my essay in *Modern Reformation*: "Restoring Eve," May 2, 2022, https://www.modernreformation.org/resources/essays/restoring-eve. They are used here with permission.
27. If covenant theology is new to you, it is well worth a deep dive. I recommend Zach Keele and Mike Brown, *Sacred Bond* (Reformed Fellowship, Inc., 2012).
28. This is known as the covenant of works, "wherein life was promised to Adam; and in him to his posterity, upon condition of perfect and personal obedience" (WCF 7.2). Adam failed to keep the covenant of works, but Christ came as the Second Adam to fulfill it in our place. We'll look at this more in chapter 3.

29. Lee-Barnewall, *Neither Complementarian nor Egalitarian*, 127.

Chapter 3: Storied

1. Portions of this chapter have been adapted from my essay in Modern Reformation: "Restoring Eve," May 2, 2022, https://www.modernreformation.org/resources/essays/restoring-eve. They are used here with permission.

2. Consider how the text is structured: God creates the man, then the woman; the serpent approaches the woman, who gives to the man; the man blames the woman, who blames the serpent; God addresses the serpent, then the woman, then man. The narrative never characterizes Adam's sin as a failure to protect Eve from the serpent. God does confront Adam for listening to the voice of his wife (Gen. 3:17), but this is presented in contrast to listening to God's voice ("of which I commanded you," also in Gen. 3:17).

3. In 2016, the ESV translators changed this translation from "Your desire shall be for your husband," to "Your desire shall be contrary to your husband." In 2025, they announced they have changed it back. I will comment on the interpretation of this verse in this chapter, but for a more detailed approach, see Kendra Dahl, "Restoring Eve," *Modern Reformation* (April/May 2022): https://www.modernreformation.org/resources/essays/restoring-eve. See also my unpublished seminary paper, "The Woman's Desire as Gracious Continuity: An Analysis of Susan Foh's Interpretation of Genesis 3:16 and an Alternate Proposal," April 2021, https://www.academia.edu/68148519/The_Womans_Desire.

4. Chrysostom, *Homilies on First Timothy*, Homily 9, https://www.newadvent.org/fathers/230609.htm.

5. Tertullian, *On the Apparel of Women*, Book 1, https://www.tertullian.org/anf/anf04/anf04-06.htm.

6. Elise Loehnen, *On Our Best Behavior: The Seven Deadly Sins and the Price Women Pay to Be Good* (The Dial Press, 2023), 3.

7. Beth Allison Barr, *The Making of Biblical Womanhood: How the Subjugation of Women Became Gospel Truth* (Brazos Press, 2021), 11–37. It's important to note that Loehnen and Barr represent very different theological approaches to this question. I don't know that Loehnen would necessarily identify herself as a Christian, and certainly not as an evangelical one. Most of her book is quite troubling. I believe Barr, on the other hand, remains within the bounds of orthodoxy. Though I don't agree with many of her exegetical or historical methods or arguments regarding the role of women in the

Notes

church, I'm sympathetic to her experience, still appreciate aspects of her work, and believe we are sisters in Christ.

8. Loehnen, *On Our Best Behavior*, 18.
9. We'll look more closely at the functions Paul is restricting here in chapter 8.
10. I believe Paul is speaking specifically of the office and corresponding functions of pastors/elders in this passage, not restricting women from teaching or exercising authority in any context. I'll expand on this in chapter 8.
11. I appreciate Kathy Keller's insight and application of these principles of biblical interpretation in *Jesus, Justice, and Gender Roles*.
12. G. K. Beale, *A New Testament Biblical Theology: The Unfolding of the Old Testament in the New* (Baker Academic, 2011), 32.
13. Benjamin L. Gladd, *From Adam and Israel to the Church: A Biblical Theology of the People of God* (IVP Academic, 2019), 12.
14. Gladd, *From Adam to Israel*, 18–19.
15. Gladd, *From Adam to Israel*, 15.
16. Gladd, *From Adam to Israel*, 15–16.
17. Gladd, *From Adam to Israel*, 23–24.
18. Ben Gladd made this observation to me in a personal conversation.
19. Abigail Favale, *The Genesis of Gender: A Christian Theory* (Ignatius Press, 2022), 46. God affirms the power of the woman's voice to influence her husband when he addresses Adam (Gen. 3:17). I think the power of a woman's voice—shown here and throughout Scripture—is so crucial that I will devote a whole chapter to it.
20. John Calvin, https://ccel.org/ccel/ calvin/calcom01/calcom01 .ix.i.html.
21. See, for example, Susan T. Foh, "What Is the Woman's Desire?," *The Westminster Theological Journal* 37, no. 3 (1975).
22. Barr, *The Making of Biblical Womanhood*, 28.
23. Joshua Van Ee, "Death and the Garden: An Examination of Original Immortality, Vegetarianism, and Animal Peace in the Hebrew Bible and Mesopotamia" (PhD diss., University of California, 2013), 170. He gives the following as examples: "the interpretation of Micah's prophecy (3:12) in Jer 26:18–19, God's statement in Ezek 33:14–15, and Jonah's complaint in Jonah 4:2."
24. People argue for a usurping desire and/or a domineering rule based on the meanings of the Hebrew words here, but these are contested translations. The Hebrew word for desire is a rare word that makes understanding its nuance difficult, but the argument that it means a "desire to usurp" is quite recent, based on the parallel language

of Genesis 3:16. However, the language of Genesis 3:16 is also difficult and not necessarily conclusive. The history of interpretation favors a more positive desire, that the woman will continue to desire her husband despite the pain of childbearing, as in the NASB (1995) translation: "In pain you will bring forth children; yet your desire will be for your husband." For more on the history of interpretation of this verse, see my unpublished paper, "The Woman's Desire: A Gracious Continuity," available at https://www.academia.edu/68148519/The_Womans_Desire. For a fuller explanation of my take here, see "Restoring Eve," https://www.modernreformation.org/resources/essays/restoring-eve. The Hebrew word for "rule" is the same word used for the sun that rules the day and the moon that rules the night (Gen. 1:16). Though the word can be used for a harsh rule, there are other Hebrew words used in these chapters that would have more clearly conveyed a shift in Adam's headship of Eve to be domineering or destructive. Instead, it appears that Moses is showing restoration and continuity. Ultimately, he's saying that the common institution of marriage will continue even amidst the impact of sin in the world.

25. Meredith G. Kline, *Kingdom Prologue Genesis Foundations for a Covenantal Worldview* (Wipf & Stock, 2006), 149.

26. Though our translations change how the phrases appear in Gen. 3:14 and 4:11, the Hebrew is the same for the serpent and Cain— "Cursed are you"—compared to Adam's—"Cursed is the ground because of you" (Gen. 3:17).

27. Timothy and Kathy Keller, *The Meaning of Marriage: Facing the Complexities of Commitment with the Wisdom of God* (Penguin Publishing Group, 2013), 44.

28. Sr. Grace Remington and Joy Clarkson, "Mary Consoles Eve," *Plough*, December 20, 2022, https://www.plough.com/en/topics/culture/holidays/christmas-readings/mary-consoles-eve.

29. Remington and Clarkson, "Mary Consoles Eve."

Chapter 4: Commissioned

Epigraph: Charlotte Bronte, *Jane Eyre*, 1847.

1. Annie Dillard, *The Writing Life* (HarperCollins, 2009).

2. For an excellent and accessible treatment of women's role in the cultural mandate and her purpose overall, read Elizabeth Garn, *Freedom to Flourish: The Rest God Offers in the Purpose He Gives You* (P&R Publishing, 2021).

NOTES

3. Kathy Keller, *Jesus, Justice, and Gender Roles* (Zondervan, 2012), Kindle location 94 of 684.

4. G. K. Beale, *The Temple and the Church's Mission: A Biblical Theology of the Dwelling Place of God*, ed. D. A. Carson, vol. 17, New Studies in Biblical Theology (InterVarsity Press, 2004), 82.

5. I say "implicit" because we don't see the word "covenant" appear in these chapters. Nonetheless, theologians have used this language to describe God's relationship to Adam and Eve for a long time. Michael Brown and Zach Keele note that the covenant of works is found as early as Augustine, is filled out with more detail and documentation in the Reformation, and is ultimately captured in Zacharias Ursinus's Larger Catechism, the Westminster Shorter Catechism, and Westminster Confession of Faith. See Michael Brown and Zach Keele, *Sacred Bond,* 41–42.

6. Michael Brown and Zach Keele, *Sacred Bond* (Reformed Fellowship, Inc., 2012), 42.

7. The Westminster Confession of Faith 19.1 says, "God gave to Adam a law, as a covenant of works, by which he bound him and all his posterity to personal, entire, exact, and perpetual obedience, promised life upon the fulfilling, and threatened death upon the breach of it, and endued him with power and ability to keep it."

8. Brown and Keele, *Sacred Bond*, 45.

9. Douglas Moo, *The Epistle to the Romans: The English Text with Introduction, Exposition and Notes,* vol. 1 (Marshall, Morgan & Scott, 1960), 315.

10. S. M. Baugh, "Covenant Theology Illustrated: Romans 5 on the Federal Headship of Adam and Christ," *Modern Reformation* 9, no. 4 (July/August 2000): 22.

11. Daniel Block, "Marriage and Family in Ancient Israel," in *Marriage and Family in the Biblical World* (InterVarsity Press, 2003), 40–44.

12. Ordination is a helpful category here, but since its application and practice varies across denominations and traditions, it's perhaps more helpful to think of the formal setting apart of a qualified man for the office of pastor or elder. This is not an informal role held by all men in the church.

13. Jen Oshman, *Cultural Counterfeits: Confronting 5 Empty Promises of Our Age and How We Were Made for So Much More* (Crossway, 2022), 39. See also Rodney Stark, *The Rise of Christianity: A Sociologist Reconsiders History* (Princeton University Press, 1996), 95.

14. Several recent works have made this point, and I commend them

to you: Glen Scrivener, *The Air We Breathe: How We All Came to Believe in Freedom, Kindness, Progress, and Equality* (Good Book Company, 2022); Rebecca McLaughlin, *Confronting Christianity: 12 Hard Questions for the World's Largest Religion* (Crossway, 2019); Tom Holland, *Dominion: How the Christian Revolution Remade the World* (Basic Books, 2019).

15. Garn, *Freedom to Flourish*, 84.

16. I first heard Jen Wilkin point out the parallels between this passage in Exodus 18 and Genesis 2:18. See "Partners in Ministry: How Men and Women Must Labor Together for the Good of the Church," *TGC Podcast*, October 4, 2024.

17. Westminster Confession of Faith, 24.2, emphasis added.

18. G. K. Beale, *The Temple and the Church's Mission: A Biblical Theology of the Dwelling Place of God*, ed. D. A. Carson, vol. 17, *New Studies in Biblical Theology* (InterVarsity Press, 2004), 81–82.

19. David VanDrunen, "Reformed Reflections on Christian Sexual Ethics," 11. This is an unpublished paper presented at the Evangelical-Catholic Dialogue of the United States, Bismarck, ND, October 2018.

20. The Greek has an article, so that it could read, "Yet she will be saved through the childbearing." Paul, having just been commenting on Genesis 1–2, could be going on to refer to Genesis 3, pointing to the unique redemptive role of mothers from Eve to Mary to bring about the promised Messiah.

21. VanDrunen, "Reformed Reflections," 13.

22. VanDrunen, "Reformed Reflections," 13–14.

23. Beale, *The Temple*, 266.

24. Beale, *The Temple*, 264.

25. Heidelberg Catechism Q&A, 32.

26. Gustaf Wingren, *Luther on Vocation* (Wipf & Stock Publishers, 2004), 10.

27. Wingren, *Luther on Vocation*, 9.

28. Blocher, *In the Beginning: The Opening Chapters of Genesis* (InterVarsity Press, 1984), 97.

29. Blocher, *In the Beginning*, 101.

30. Louise Perry, *The Case Against the Sexual Revolution* (Polity, 2022), 30.

Chapter 5: Vulnerable

Epigraph: Betty Smith, *A Tree Grows in Brooklyn*, 1943.

1. "Dru Katrina Sjodin, 1981–2003," National Sex Offender Public Website, https://www.nsopw.gov/about-dru.

Notes

2. Louise Perry, *The Case Against the Sexual Revolution* (Polity, 2022), 27.
3. Throughout history, this verse has been used to argue for a broader application of women's weakness, meaning she is physically, emotionally, spiritually, intellectually, and psychologically inferior to men. On the roots of this thinking, see Rachel Green Miller's helpful chapter, "The General Inferiority of the Female Sex," in *Beyond Authority and Submission: Women and Men in Marriage, Church, and Society* (P&R, 2019), 47–60.
4. Perry, *A Case*, 29.
5. It's important to note that Peter is not suggesting women should stay in abusive marriages. The context of suffering in 1 Peter is for the gospel's sake. As Justin and Lindsey Holcomb write, "Scripture shows us a complex and multifaceted view of human suffering, and so we must not be simplistic in our counsel to ourselves and to others who face unjust suffering," because God will never "[call] us into violence if it can be avoided." Justin S. Holcomb and Lindsey A. Holcomb, *Is It My Fault? Hope and Healing for Those Suffering Domestic Violence* (Moody, 2014), 128.
6. This paragraph is adapted from "The Evil Queen," an entry in my Christmas devotional, "The Promised Seed," available as a PDF download at Core Christianity. It is used here with permission.
7. Jen Wilkin, "Fight Like a Girl," Breakaway Ministries, February 24, 2015, https://subsplash.com/breakaway/messages/mi/+b7ab1a.
8. Notice the language that starts this narrative of female bravery—"*But* the midwives feared God and did not do as the king of Egypt commanded them, but let the male children live" (Ex. 1:17).
9. Wilkin, "Fight."
10. We'll look more closely at this passage in the next chapter.
11. Elisabeth Elliot, "The Essence of Femininity," *Crossway*, June 16, 2015, https://www.crossway.org/articles/the-essence-of-femininity/.
12. Elliot uses wording like this in "Essence," https://www.crossway.org/articles/the-essence-of-femininity/.
13. Elliot, "Essence," https://www.crossway.org/articles/the-essence-of-femininity/.
14. I'm quoting from a transcript of Jen Wilkin's talk at Breakaway Ministries, "Fight Like a Girl."
15. Wilkin, "Fight."
16. Jenny Rae Armstrong, "Making Space for the Feminine Voice," https://www.jennyraearmstrong.com/2012/06/07/making-space-for-the-feminine-voice-rerun/.
17. I'm not suggesting birth control is necessarily a bad development for

A PLACE FOR YOU

women; I'm simply observing that this sexual freedom comes at a cost.

18. Mary Harrington, "Counting the Cost of Progress," *Plough*, May 1, 2023, https://www.plough.com/en/topics/justice/social-justice/counting-the-cost-of-progress.

19. Chris Williamson, "The Harsh Truth About Female 'Empowerment'," *Modern Wisdom*, December 4, 2023 https://www.youtube.com/watch?v=HAmQ7Tcrh6A.

20. Wilkin, "Fight."

Chapter 6: Quiet

Epigraph: Louisa May Alcott, *Little Women*, 1868–69.

1. Claudia Hammond, "Prattle of the Sexes: Do Women Talk More than Men?," BBC, November 11, 2013, https://www.bbc.com/future/article/20131112-do-women-talk-more-than-men; Jessica Schrader, "Do Women Really Talk More than Men? What's the evidence?," *Psychology Today*, October 10, 2019, https://www.psychologytoday.com/intl/blog/marriage-equals/201910/do-women-really-talk-more-men.

2. "Do Women Talk More than Men?," *Harvard School of Public Health*, July 23, 2014, https://hsph.harvard.edu/news/do-women-talk-more-than-men/.

3. Deborah Tannen, "The Truth About How Much Women Talk—and Whether Men Listen," *Time*, June 28, 2017, https://time.com/4837536/do-women-really-talk-more/; see also "Which Is the Most Talkative Gender? It All Depends," Eureka Alert, November 8, 2007, https://www.eurekalert.org/news-releases/710363.

4. Deborah Tannen, "The Power of Talk: Who Gets Heard and Why," *Harvard Business Review* (September–October 1995): https://hbr.org/1995/09/the-power-of-talk-who-gets-heard-and-why.

5. Tannen, "The Truth."

6. Dimitrije Curcic, "How Many Words Does the Average Person Say a Day?," WordsRated, November 7, 2023, https://wordsrated.com/how-many-words-does-the-average-person-say-a-day/.

7. Katie Reilly, "Why 'Nevertheless, She Persisted' Is the Theme for This Year's Women's History Month," *Time*, March 1, 2018, https://time.com/5175901/elizabeth-warren-nevertheless-she-persisted-meaning/.

8. Reilly, "Nevertheless."

9. Reilly, "Nevertheless."

Notes

10. "Report of the Ad Interim Committee on Women Serving in the Ministry of the Church to the Forty-Fifth General Assembly of the Presbyterian Church in America," 17.

11. PCA Report, 18.

12. PCA Report, 13, suggests two possible contexts Paul could have in mind here: "Specifically, when Paul says women must remain silent, he means either silent by not preaching (espoused by Calvin, and other older interpreters) or he means silent during the testing of prophecy (espoused by Carson, Grudem, and more recent interpreters)."

13. PCA Report, 20.

14. PCA Report, 14.

15. PCA Report, 14.

16. PCA Report, 18 (n26).

17. Rodney Stark, *The Rise of Christianity: A Sociologist Reconsiders History* (Princeton University Press, 1996), 99–100.

18. Stark, *The Rise*, 99.

19. Abigail Favale, *The Genesis of Gender* (Ignatius Press, 2022), 46.

20. PCA Report, 8.

21. Lily Rothman, "A Cultural History of Mansplaining," *Atlantic*, November 1, 2012, https://www.theatlantic.com/sexes/archive/2012/11/a-cultural-history-of-mansplaining/264380/; Liana M. Kreamer et al., "Virtual Voices: Exploring Individual Differences in Chat and Verbal Participation in Virtual Meetings," *Journal of Vocational Behavior* 152 (August 2024): https://www.sciencedirect.com/science/article/abs/pii/S0001879124000563; Anne Gulland, "Men Dominate Conference Q&A Sessions—Including Online Ones," *Nature*, December 1, 2022, https://www.nature.com/articles/d41586-022-04241-y.

Chapter 7: Limited

Epigraph: Lin-Manuel Miranda, "Surface Pressure," *Encanto*, Walt Disney Records, 2021.

1. Betty Friedan, *The Feminine Mystique: The Classic That Sparked a Feminist Revolution* (Thread, 2021).

2. Brigid Schulte, *Overwhelmed: Work, Love and Play When No One Has the Time* (Bloomsbury Publishing, 2014) 75–76.

3. Jessica Valenti, *Why Have Kids?: A New Mom Explores the Truth About Parenting and Happiness* (Amazon Publishing, 2018), 40–41.

4. Randi Olin, "Motherwell Talks to Best-Selling Author Eve Rodsky," *MotherWell*, March 15, 2020, https://motherwellmag.

com/2020/03/15/motherwell-talks-to-best-selling-author-eve-rodsky/.

5. Olin, "Motherwell."

6. Jason Pierce, "Betty Friedan and the Women's Movement," Bill of Rights Institute, https://billofrightsinstitute.org/essays/betty-friedan-and-the-womens-movement.

7. Anne Helen Petersen, "How Millennials Became the Burnout Generation," BuzzFeed News, January 5, 2019, https://www.buzzfeednews.com/article/annehelenpetersen/millennials-burnout-generation-debt-work.

8. Ryan Pendell, "Millennials Are Burning Out" Gallup, July 19, 2018: https://www.gallup.com/workplace/237377/millennials-burning.aspx.

9. Petersen, "Millennials."

10. US Department of Health and Human Services, "Our Epidemic of Loneliness and Isolation: The US Surgeon General's Advisory on the Healing Effects of Social Connection and Community," 2023, https://www.hhs.gov/sites/default/files/surgeon-general-social-connection-advisory.pdf.

11. HHS, "Our Epidemic," 8–9.

12. For a deeper dive into the beauty of God-ordained limits, see Ashley Hales, *A Spacious Life: Trading Hustle and Hurry for the Goodness of Limits* (InterVarsity Press, 2021).

13. Sam Allberry makes a similar observation, attributing it to Rebecca McLaughlin, in his breakout session at the TGC 2021 Women's Conference, "Don't Waste Your Singleness," April 10, 2021, https://www.youtube.com/watch?v=ggWPiGtWmX8.

14. Shelley E. Taylor et al., "Biobehavioral Responses to Stress in Females: Tend-and-Befriend, Not Fight-or-Flight," *Psychological Review* 107, no. 3 (July 2000): 411–19.

15. Taylor et al., "Biobehavioral," 411.

16. Taylor et al., "Biobehavioral," 411.

17. Taylor et al., "Biobehavioral," 419.

18. Deborah Tannen, "The Power of Talk: Who Gets Heard and Why," *Harvard Business Review* (September–October 1995): https://hbr.org/1995/09/the-power-of-talk-who-gets-heard-and-why.

19. It's a gift when biological family can provide this network, but I think it's important for us to see that God calls us to a more expansive view of family life and that we have an important place within it.

20. Paul Miller, *A Praying Life: Connecting with God in a Distracting World* (NavPress, 2017), 49.

Notes

21. Zack Eswine, *Recovering Eden: The Gospel According to Ecclesiastes* (P&R Publishing, 2014), 105.

Chapter 8: Secondary

Epigraph: Peter Brown, *The Wild Robot* (Little, Brown Books for Young Readers, 2023).

1. Dan Cable, "What You Should Follow Instead of Your Passion," *Harvard Business Review* (November 24, 2020): https://hbr.org/2020/11/what-you-should-follow-instead-of-your-passion.
2. Brigid Schulte, *Overwhelmed*, 78.
3. Linda Peacore, "Vocation and the Christian Life," Fuller Seminary, October 6, 2010, https://www.fuller.edu/next-faithful-step/classes/cf565/vocation-and-the-christian-life/.
4. Peacore, "Vocation."
5. Peacore, "Vocation."
6. Peacore, "Vocation."
7. Tim Keller, *Generous Justice: How God's Grace Makes Us Just* (Riverhead Books, 2010), 89–92.
8. Peacore, "Vocation."
9. This paragraph reflects the insight of my seminary classmate and friend, Rev. Christian McArthur. I'm grateful for his sharpening and input as I worked through the content for this chapter.
10. Though people dispute the meaning of authority in these passages, I find the arguments for "exercise authority" by Al Wolters, "The Meaning of Αὐθεντέω," in *Women in the Church: An Interpretation and Application of 1 Timothy 2:9–15*, 3rd ed. (ed. Andreas J. Köstenberger and Thomas R. Schreiner, Crossway, 2016), 64–115, and Köstenberger, "A Complex Sentence," 117–61, to be more compelling than "domineer" or "usurp" per Belleville, "Teaching," 205–23. See Linda L. Belleville, "Teaching and Usurping Authority: 1 Timothy 2:11–15," 205–22, in *Discovering Biblical Equality: Complementarity Without Hierarchy*. Edited by Ronald W. Pierce and Rebecca Merrill Groothuis (InterVarsity Press, 2005) and Andreas J. Köstenberger, "A Complex Sentence: The Syntax of 1 Timothy 2:12," 117–62 in *Women in the Church: An Interpretation and Application of 1 Timothy 2:9–15*, 3rd ed. Edited by Andreas J. Köstenberger and Thomas R. Schreiner (Crossway, 2016).
11. Heidelberg Catechism Q&A 83.
12. Some do make this argument today, arguing women can preach under the authority of elders. My convictions don't align with this view, but I understand why some find it compelling. See John

A PLACE FOR YOU

Dickson, *Hearing Her Voice: A Case for Women Giving Sermons* (Zondervan, 2014).

13. Though women are not called to be elders who preside over church discipline, that doesn't mean they can't be a valuable resource to pastors and elders walking through difficult cases. When discipline and shepherding cases involve a woman, wise pastors will leverage the godly women in their congregation to gain perspective, help, and support. Though Paul issues these instructions, he also models including women as partners in ministry (Rom. 16:1–16; Phil. 4:3) and commends the role of godly women in the life of the church (Titus 2:3–5; 1 Tim. 5:9–10).

14. This is also the conclusion promoted by Kathy Keller, *Jesus, Justice, and Gender Roles*, location 245 of 684.

15. Keller, *Jesus, Justice, and Gender Roles*, location 364 of 684.

16. Matt Smethurst, *Deacons: How They Serve and Strengthen the Church (9Marks: Building Healthy Churches)* (Crossway, 2021), 24.

17. Smethurst, *Deacons*, 25.

18. Michael Kruger observes this about Romans 16 and expands on the necessity of women in ministry in his excellent breakout session at the 2024 TGC Women's Conference, "Why We Need Women in Ministry," https://www.youtube.com/watch?v=iVnn-HdoS3Nk&t=2s.

19. PCA Report, 57.

20. Jen Pollock Michel, "A Message to John MacArthur: The Bible Calls Both Men and Women to 'Go Home'," *Christianity Today*, October 24, 2019, https://www.christianitytoday.com/2019/10/john-macarthur-bible-invites-both-men-women-go-home/.

21. Parts of the following section come from my essay, "Why You Should Preach the 'Family Gospel'," Core Christianity, used with permission. Kendra Dahl, posted August 30, 2021, https://core-christianity.com/resources/articles/why-you-should-preach-the-family-gospel.

22. I love this metaphor from Mary Harrington shared in a recent newsletter: "We have a lot of frayed social fabric to make up. Literal weaving has historically always been one of women's core skills; I firmly believe the metaphorical kind has, too." "New Year's Resolution: Bring Back the Aunties," Mary Harrington, December 31, 2024, https://www.maryharrington.co.uk/p/new-years-resolution-bring-back-the.

23. My husband has written an excellent booklet that provides a helpful guide for decision-making, including wise questions to ask when you're considering whether you should stay or go. These

Notes

ideas come from him (pp. 41–42), and I recommend the whole resource! Jordan Dahl, *What Is God's Will for Me?*, https://store .solamedia.org/products/what-is-gods-will-for-me; Gavin Ortlund's book *Finding the Right Hills to Die On* (Crossway, 2020) may also be a useful resource as you consider if your differing convictions require you to find a new church community.

Closing Thoughts

1. Louisa May Alcott, *Little Women*, 1868–69.
2. I also have the neatest little man growing up under my roof! Love you, Maximus!

You finished reading!

Did this book help you in some way? If so, please consider writing an honest review wherever you purchase your books. Your review gets this book into the hands of more readers and helps us continue to create biblically faithful resources.

Moody Publishers' books help fund the training of students for ministry around the world.

The **Moody Bible Institute** is one of the most well-known Christian institutions in the world, training thousands of young people to faithfully serve Christ wherever He calls them. And when you buy and read a book from Moody Publishers, you're helping make that vital ministry training possible.

Continue to dive into the Word, *anytime, anywhere.*

Find what you need to take your next step in your walk with Christ: from uplifting music to sound preaching, our programs are designed to help you right when you need it.

Download the **Moody Radio App** and start listening today!

 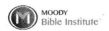